WEARABLE ART WITH SONDRA

Over 75 Fun and Easy Craft Projects to Make and Wear

Sondra Clark

PRIMA HOME
An Imprint of Prima Publishing
3000 Lava Ridge Court • Roseville, CA 95661
(800) 632-8676 • www.primalifestyles.com

Interior illustrations by Emily Eklund and Melanie Merz
Interior Design by Lori Bulay

Library of Congress Cataloging-in-Publication Data

Clark, Sondra.
    Wearable art with Sondra : over 75 fun and easy craft projects to make and wear / Sondra Clark.
       p.   cm.
    ISBN: 0-7615-2540-8
    1. Handicraft—Juvenile literature. 2. Wearable art—Juvenile literature. 3. Clothing and dress—Juvenile literature. 4. Dress accessories—Juvenile literature. 5. Jewelry making—Juvenile literature. [1. Handicraft. 2. Wearable art. 3. Clothing and dress. 4. Dress accessories. 5. Jewelry making.] I. Title.

TT160.C5624 2000
745.5—dc21   00-057438

00 01 02 03 04 HH 10 9 8 7 6 5 4 3 2 1
Printed in the United States of America

Visit us online at www.primalifestyles.com

AUTHOR'S NOTE

Mom,

Thank you for helping me write this book and make the crafts. Thank you also for helping me market the book and for getting me on TV shows. And thank you for being a wonderful mother.

Love,
Sondra

CONTENTS

Chapter Four: COOL CLOTHES FROM HEAD TO TOE — 107

ACKNOWLEDGMENTS

Obviously, as a ten-year-old, I couldn't write this book without some help from adults. I want to thank my literary agent, Linda Konner, who has helped me get two books published. She normally gets professional-looking manuscripts from her authors. From me, she gets samples of painted T-shirts, dried carrot necklaces, and decorated hats.

I want to thank my dad, who always helps out with my craft projects. He gets the hard job of building shelves and hanging giant paint holders from the wall so I can store my craft supplies.

Thanks also to everyone at Prima Publishing who let me talk to them on conference calls and helped put this book together. I got to do the fun things like make all the sample projects while they did the nitty-gritty work of turning the written pages into an actual book.

Sondra has chosen Childcare International (*www.childcare-intl.org*) to receive a portion of sales from each of her books sold.

INTRODUCTION

My mom and I had great fun writing this book, and we hope you'll have fun using it. Take advantage of being able to get your hands messy—and not get yelled at—and to make something however you want, without your teacher grading it. You can even make someone a personalized birthday gift if you're short on money. Whatever you decide to do is up to you, but we've given you great ideas and instructions for taking boring items laying around your house and turning them into fun fashions you can wear.

Before you get started, here are a few tips:

■ Always check with an adult before starting a project. You need permission before you sponge-paint your dad's favorite T-shirt!

■ If using a hot glue gun or iron, have an adult help you or at least stand right next to you. That way you'll be less likely to burn yourself.

■ Spread old newspapers on your work surface. Your parents would rather you get paint and glue on the paper instead of the dining room table. If you have an old vinyl shower curtain or picnic tablecloth, that works well to cover your surface also. Just wipe the covering off when you're finished, and it can be used over and over again.

■ As you decide on a project, make sure you have all the supplies. It's frustrating to get excited about making something and then realize you are missing an important item.

(Most of the ideas in this book are designed for you to be creative. If you don't have thin ribbon, yarn will probably work also. Feel free to substitute items.)

✿ Don't feel your project has to look picture-perfect. Part of the fun of wearable art is that each item has its own unique look. Hey, expensive boutiques charge high prices for one-of-a-kind items!

✿ Next time you have a birthday, ask for some basic craft supplies. Fabric paint, good quality brushes, stencils, and some fancy buttons go a long way in creating wearable art projects.

✿ This may not be the most exciting tip, but . . . clean up your mess! We all know how fun it is to get involved in a project made with beads, or designing a purse. Just remember to put your supplies away and leave your work area clean. Besides, when you want to start another project, it's easier when you can begin with a clean space. Safety is an issue also. You don't want to trip over items you've tossed on the floor.

✿ If using paints, it's a good idea to wear an old T-shirt or paint smock to protect your good clothes.

✿ Looking for an easy way to keep track of your craft supplies? Buy an inexpensive, plastic hanging shoe rack. Each separate compartment can hold glue, scissors, pipe cleaners, or whatever else you have.

✿ If you want to make small polka dots on an item, just dip the hard end of your paintbrush in paint. Dab the end on your project and you'll have even-sized polka dots.

✿ Most of all, have fun! The idea behind any arts and crafts project is to enjoy the creative process. Experiment with different-sized beads. Try mixing two colors of paint together to create a brand new color. Glue buttons on a headband and see if you like the design. There's no right or wrong way to create wearable art projects. Whatever you design will be extra special because *you* made it!

Here are some items to start collecting for your wearable art projects:

Sponges

Paintbrushes

Adhesive-backed paper

Fabric scraps

Fabric glue

Fabric crayons (Crayola brand gives excellent results.)

Scissors

Permanent markers

Washable glue (This glue lets you glue lace and trim to fabric. When you wash the clothes, the glue still sticks tight!)

Popsicle sticks

Empty yogurt containers

Styrofoam meat trays (Use these for mixing paint.)

Empty egg cartons (great for storing beads and buttons)

Rubberstamps

Scraps of yarn

Assorted ribbons (Save ribbons from birthday presents.)

Felt

Craft foam

Buttons (Even plain buttons look "fancy" if you stack 2 or 3 together.)

Beads (Go to garage sales and buy inexpensive necklaces. Cut them apart and reuse the beads.)

Scrap pieces of cardboard

Old newspapers

Plastic shower curtain or tablecloth (used, of course!)

T-shirts, sweatshirts, old jeans, etc. (Even if the clothes have holes or tears, you can use them.)

Different-shaped pasta

Old or scratched hair barrettes and headbands

Plastic visors

Cotton hats

Wiggle eyes

The following are some items you probably don't have around the house. You may want to purchase them if you plan on making a wide variety of wearable art projects:

Delta Ceramcoat Textile Medium: This product transforms acrylic paint into a washable fabric paint. Order this by calling (800) 423-4135.

Loew-Cornell: This company sells a round bristled Splatter Paintbrush that lets you make an even "splatter" effect on clothes or other items. Contact them at (201) 836-7070 or *www.loew-cornell.com*.

EZ Dots: This cute, small plastic tool lets you easily make four different-sized dots. Order it by calling (909) 944-8613 or visiting their Web site at *www.ezdotz.com*.

Color ToolBox Stylus: Imagine a toothbrush with a foam pad at each end. Heat the black foam tip with a lightbulb for 20 seconds. Press down on any textured surface. You've just made a custom stamp. Call (800) 448-4862 or visit *www.clearsnap.com* for more information on this tool.

Wash-Out! Paint: You can use this paint to decorate a shirt. When you get tired of the design, wash the shirt to remove the paint. Then start over again. Check it out at *www.go-inkblots.com*.

Chapter One

ARTSY ACCESSORIES

FLOWER POWER SUNGLASSES

Sondra Says:

"After you decorate your sunglasses, it's fun to play with the left-over clay. The slices turn into colorful beads if you roll them into small balls and poke holes in them before they dry."

Official Supply List

1 package of cut-and-slice polymer clay, any design (this clay comes in rolls with various designs that appear when you slice the clay)

Sharp knife

Cookie sheet

Oven

Super Glue or Krazy Glue

Sunglasses

Ready . . . Set . . . Create!

1. Warm the clay according to the package directions.
2. Slice the clay into ⅛-inch slices.
3. Cut a few slices in halves or fourths for different designs.
4. Place the slices on the cookie sheet.
5. Have an adult bake the slices in the oven at 130 degrees F for 20 to 25 minutes.
6. Remember … these are not to be eaten!
7. When the clay is baked, remove from the oven and cool.
8. Use the glue to attach the baked clay pieces to your sunglasses.

A tip from Sondra:

Make sure to use a sharp knife to cut the roll of clay into slices. Ask an adult for help. You can also slide a piece of dental floss under the roll of clay. Bring the ends of the floss together over the roll and then criss-cross them. The floss will slice the clay evenly.

Check out this Web site for lots of ideas
on how to use polymer clay: *www.sculpey.com*.

HEART-FLOWER VISOR

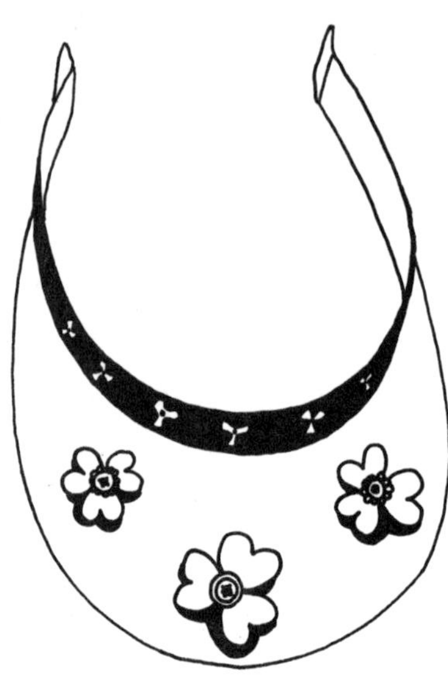

Sondra Says:

"This is an easy way to turn a plain visor into something bright and shiny."

Official Supply List

Permanent markers or paint

Plain-colored plastic sun visor

Small paintbrushes (if using paint)

Scissors

Scrap pieces of felt or craft foam, or precut small foam
   heart shapes

Glue

Buttons

Small shiny beads

Ready . . . Set . . . Create!

1. Using the markers or paint, color the top band on the visor.

2. Decide how many flowers you want on the visor.

3. Cut 3 hearts out of the felt for each flower (or use the precut foam heart shapes).

4. Glue 3 hearts on the visor with their pointed ends touching. This forms a flower.

5. If you want, use a permanent green marker to draw a stem and leaves from each flower.

6. Glue a button in the center of your petals.

7. Add a shiny bead on top of the button.

8. Glue additional shiny beads on the colored band you painted.

9. Go outside and let the sun shine down on your sparkly visor.

A tip from Sondra:
To make it easy to glue on the beads, just dip a toothpick into the glue, then dab the toothpick where you want to attach the bead. This saves your fingers from getting sticky.

Have an adult call Economy Handicrafts
at (800) 216-1601 and ask for their free catalog
of inexpensive craft supplies.

SINGING IN THE RAIN UMBRELLA

Sondra Says:

"You can decorate your umbrella on a sunny day so it is ready the next time it rains."

Official Supply List

Plain-colored umbrella (lighter colors work best)

Clip art or drawings*

White paper

Black marker

Tape

Hot glue gun

Glue sticks (use colored sticks for a pretty design)

Fabric paint

Paintbrush

Ready . . . Set . . . Create!

1. Open your umbrella so it is easy to paint.
2. Find clip art or simple drawings of teddy bears, butter-flies, animals, etc. You can use your own designs also.*
3. Outline the picture on white paper with a black marker.
4. Tape the picture on the underside of the umbrella, so you can see the design through the fabric.
5. With an adult nearby, use the glue gun to outline the design on top of the umbrella. If you use colored glue sticks, you'll get a more colorful design.
6. The glue will leave thin "threads" of glue, like a spider web, in some places. Simply pull off the loose threads.
7. Use fabric paint to paint inside the glue lines. It's almost like Paint By Number.
8. Let the paint dry.
9. Repeat the process for as many designs as you want on your umbrella.

*If you can't think of creative designs, use the patterns on page 174.

A tip from Sondra:
Many glue guns now come with "low-melt" glue sticks. These aren't quite as hot as the high temperature ones, but you still need to be careful not to burn your fingers.

If you don't want to buy bottles of fabric paint, try this trick. Simply get a bottle of Delta Ceramcoat Textile Medium. You can mix it with any acrylic paint, and it turns into permanent fabric paint!

JEAN POCKET PURSES

Sondra Says:

"This is a great way to get use out of jeans that are too small for you to wear."

Official Supply List

Scissors

Old pair of jeans

Iron and ironing board

Iron-on appliqués

Needle and thread

About 24 inches of ribbon or cord

Ready . . . Set . . . Create!

1. Carefully cut out the back pocket from your jeans, cutting both the pocket and the fabric underneath it.

2. Trim the top fabric so it meets the top of the pocket.

3. With an adult's help, use the iron to secure several appliqués onto the pocket side of the piece.

4. Let cool.

5. Using the needle and thread, sew one end of the ribbon or cord on one of the top corners of the pocket.

6. Sew the other end of the ribbon to the other top corner. This makes your handle for the purse.

7. Slip the purse over your shoulder and get ready to go shopping!

8. Some jeans have smaller pockets set inside a larger pocket. Cut the smaller pocket out and make a matching purse for a doll.

A tip from Sondra:

If you want, sew a piece of Velcro to the top center of the pocket to make a "clasp" that stops things from falling out.

Design Originals offers a series of *Can Do Crafts* books for all ages. Look at their Web site at *www.d-originals.com* or ask an adult to order their catalog for you by calling (800) 877-7820.

BEADED BELT

(extra quick and easy)

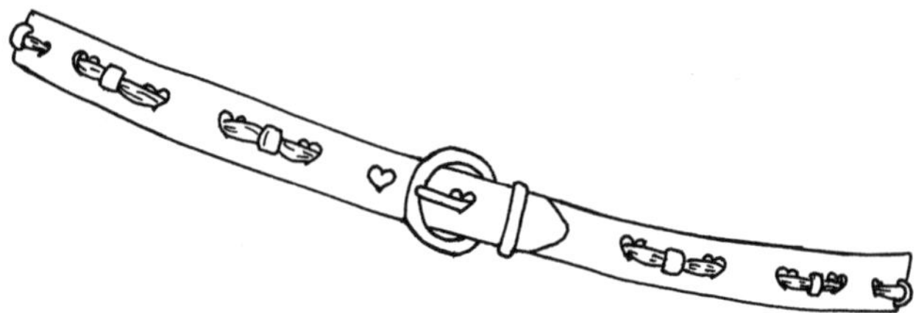

Sondra Says:

"You can use one belt and change the beads and ribbons as often as you want to match different outfits."

Official Supply List

Tape

1½ yards of ½-inch wide cloth ribbon

Belt with evenly spaced holes

Beads (the same number as the holes in the belt)

Ready . . . Set . . . Create!

1. Tightly wrap about an inch of tape around one end of the ribbon. This forms a "needle" to make weaving easier.

2. Begin at one end of the belt, on the underneath side. Bring the ribbon up through the first hole.

3. Add a bead to the ribbon and then go down through the next hole.

4. Repeat by weaving the ribbon in and out of the holes, adding a bead each time.

5. When completed, tie each loose end of the ribbon to the woven ribbon underneath the belt. That's all there is to it!

A tip from Sondra:
If you can't find a belt that already has holes, ask an adult to use a paper punch and put holes in a thin plastic or leather belt.

It's fun to make your own beads. Get ideas from the book *Beads,* by Judy Ann Sadler (Kids Can Press).

RIBBON TRINKET BAGS

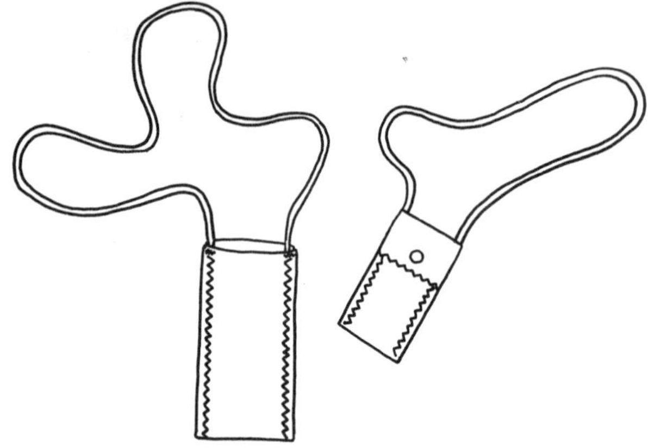

Sondra Says:

"I like going to the fabric store and picking out special ribbons to make these bags. Then it's fun and easy to use the sewing machine to sew the sides together."

Official Supply List

10 to 12 inches of wide ribbon (at least 3 inches wide)

Iron and ironing board

20 to 25 inches of ¼-inch or ½-inch ribbon in a color that
   goes well with your wide ribbon

Sewing machine (with zigzag stitch, if possible)

Ready . . . Set . . . Create!

1. With an adult nearby, fold ½ inch of each end of the wide ribbon to its underside and iron it so it stays. This gives you a smooth top edge for your trinket bag.
2. Fold the wide ribbon in half, with the "pretty" side of the ribbon on the outside.
3. Carefully lay about 1 inch of the thin ribbon down inside the bag, in the middle of the two wide ribbon pieces on each side where they meet the fabric. This will be the handle.
4. Use the sewing machine to sew up one side of the wide ribbon, making sure the thin ribbon is sewn in also.
5. Repeat on the other side.

A tip from Sondra:
If you don't have a sewing machine, no problem.
You can sew the sides by hand or use a strong
craft glue.

Here's a fun product! The ReCapper is a snap-on lid that turns an empty 2-liter plastic bottle into a great storage container. Check it out at *www.starline.com.*

MANICURED GLOVES

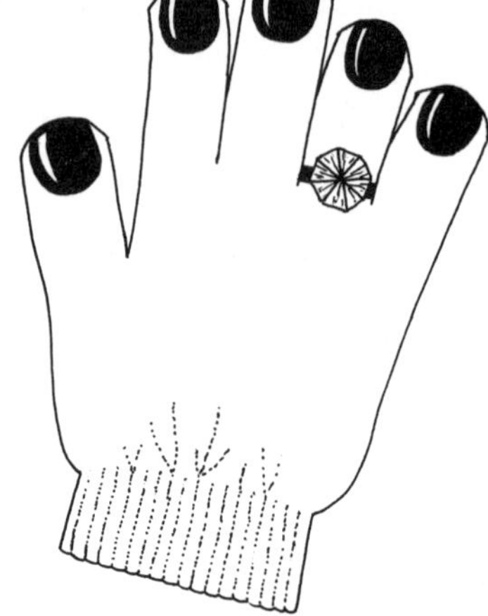

Sondra Says:

"When you wear these gloves, people will ask where you got your fancy manicure."

Official Supply List

Scrap cardboard

Pair of gloves

Red permanent marker

Red and silver or gold fabric paint

Paintbrush

Glue

Sparkly bead

Ready . . . Set . . . Create!

1. Slip small pieces of cardboard into each finger of the glove (this stops the paint from soaking through).
2. Use the red permanent marker to draw an outline of a fingertip on each finger of the glove.
3. Squeeze some red paint on a scrap piece of cardboard.
4. Use the paintbrush to paint the fingernail outlines a solid red.
5. Use silver or gold to draw a ring band on one finger.
6. Let the gloves dry.
7. Glue the sparkly bead on top of the ring line to complete your elegant hand.

A tip from Sondra:
Fabric paint is permanent. That's great for wearable art projects, but be careful not to get any on your good clothes.

Delta Paints offers Glitter Fabric Paint in shiny colors. Look at their Web site: *www.deltacrafts.com.*

FANCY SHOELACES

(extra quick and easy)

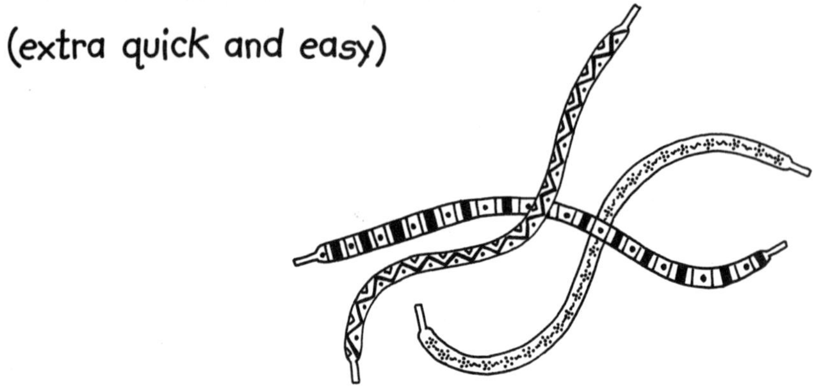

Sondra Says:

"These shoelaces will make a wild addition to your Easy Tie-Dye Tennis Shoes on page 110."

Official Supply List

Solid-color shoelaces

Tape

Newspaper

Fabric paint

Toothpicks or thin paintbrushes

Permanent markers

Ready . . . Set . . . Create!

1. Lay your shoelaces on a flat surface.
2. Tape each end down so the shoelaces are stretched tight.
3. Slide a piece of newspaper under the shoelaces so you don't get paint on your work surface.
4. Create a design with fabric paint on your shoelaces (some designs might be: polka dots, black zebra stripes, or tiny flowers). You can use toothpicks to paint intricate patterns with fabric paint, or simply use permanent markers.

A tip from Sondra:

If you want to make "perfect" polka dots, simply use the plastic end of a paintbrush. Dip the end into the paint and dab it on the shoelace. You'll have a great-looking polka dot.

You can get low-cost beads, buttons, and sequins from Creative Crafts. Their free catalog is available by calling (800) 666-0767 (ask an adult to call) or visiting their Web site at *www.discoverywatch.com*.

SMILEY-FACE GLOVES

(extra quick and easy)

Sondra Says:

"You can't help but smile when you wear these 'happy' gloves."

Official Supply List

Scrap cardboard

Pair of smooth-knit gloves (any color but yellow)

Yellow fabric paint

Paper plate

Chapstick cap (or other cap about ½ inch in diameter)

Black permanent marker

Ready . . . Set . . . Create!

1. Slide a piece of cardboard inside each finger of the gloves. This keeps the paint from soaking through.

2. Pour yellow paint on the paper plate.

3. Dip the Chapstick cap in the paint, solid side down.

4. Stamp the paint on the tip of each glove finger. If you want, stamp a circle in the center of the glove, too.

5. Let paint dry.

6. Use the permanent marker to draw a smiley face on each yellow circle.

7. Be happy!

A tip from Sondra:
If you want, put smiley faces on both sides of the gloves. Then you'll see a smile no matter where your hand is. Make sure to let the paint dry completely on one side before doing the other side.

Look at the Girls Incorporated Web site
for hundreds of ideas on things girls can make or do:
www.girlsinc.org.

BEADED BOW HAT

Sondra Says:

"This is an easy way to make an ordinary hat look like it's decorated with expensive bows."

Official Supply List

Scissors

½-inch-wide ribbon, 4 inches for each bow you make (ribbon with wire edges makes crisper bows)

Washable glue (available in most craft stores)

10 to 15 pony beads (one bead for each bow you make)

Wool (or other fabric) hat (a plain color shows off the beads best)

Needle and thread

Ready . . . Set . . . Create!

1. Cut ribbon into 4-inch lengths.
2. Glue the ends of each length together so you have a "doughnut."
3. Before the glue dries, slip the ribbon through the bead, so the bead is in the middle. (If the glue dries, the ribbon gets stiff and may be hard to push through the pony beads.)
4. Smooth out the edges of the ribbon. It should look like a bow.
5. Sew the beaded bows on your hat.

A tip from Sondra:
You can use this same technique to make bows and then sew them on to clothes or other styles of hats.

American Girl magazine offers colorful and fun craft projects in every issue. You can check it out in the library or have an adult call (800) 845-0005 for subscription information.

BEADED SCARF

Sondra Says:

"Fleece is great to use because you don't have to sew the edges. It also comes in bright colors."

Official Supply List

⅓ yard of fleece

Scissors

15 to 20 pony beads of your choice

Ready . . . Set . . . Create!

1. At each end of the fleece, cut into the fabric about four inches, about 20 times on each end. This gives a fringed look.

2. String a pony bead over one piece of fringe. Push the bead to the top of the slit.

3. Slip another bead on the same piece of fringe. About halfway up the piece of fringe, tie the fringe in a knot around the bead. This keeps both beads from slipping off the fabric.

4. Repeat the process, putting beads on as many pieces of fringe as you want.

5. Wait for a cold day and wrap yourself up in this cozy scarf.

A tip from Sondra:
To make it easier to slip the bead over the fleece, cut the bottom edge of each piece of fringe at an angle. The pointed edge slips into the bead easier.

Check out the colorful and easy-to-use Jangle Web site, *www.jangle.com*. The section under Jangle Jr. shows many creative craft projects.

SPARKLING VISOR

(extra quick and easy)

Sondra Says:

"When you wear this visor outside at night, you'll really shine whenever lights hits it!"

Official Supply List

Scissors

Reflective tape (You'll be surprised at how many colors and patterns of reflective tape are available at most home improvement stores.)

Plastic visor

Ready . . . Set . . . Create!

1. Cut the reflective tape into various shapes, such as squiggly lines, hearts, or triangles.*

2. Pull off the protective backing from each piece of reflective tape and stick the tape on the visor.

3. Have an adult go outside with you and watch how your visor reflects the light.

A tip from Sondra:

If you have extra pieces of reflective tape, put them on your bike or bike helmet for extra safety.

CraftDesigns sells unique organizers
for storing all your craft supplies. Removable bins
and a clear lid help you keep track of all your beads,
thread, and buttons. See *www.akro-mils.com*.

MAGIC DESIGN BELT

(extra quick and easy)

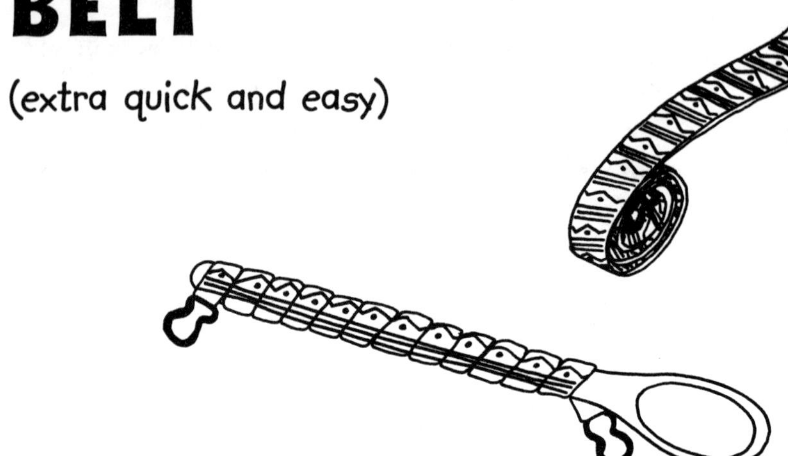

Sondra Says:

"This technique to make designs also works if you want to decorate your shoelaces."

Official Supply List

Masking tape

Cotton or other fabric belt (a solid, light color)

Wooden spoon with a long handle

Permanent markers or fabric pens

Ready . . . Set . . . Create!

1. Use the tape to attach one end of the belt to the wooden spoon handle.

2. Wrap the belt around the handle. Make sure the edges of the fabric touch, but don't overlap.

3. When the belt is securely wrapped, tape the other end.

4. Sometimes it helps to have a friend or adult hold the wrapped spoon while you do the next step.

5. Use the markers or fabric pens to draw straight lines or designs on the belt. Begin at the top and draw down to the bottom of the spoon, as shown in the illustration. You can make polka dots, zigzags, or wavy lines. Use several colors if you want a bright belt.

6. When your design is finished, pull off the tape and unwind the belt. You'll be amazed at the symmetrical pattern.

A tip from Sondra:
To understand this technique, practice by cutting a piece of paper the same size as your belt. Wrap the paper around the spoon and make some designs on it before you actually draw on the belt.

Need places to store your craft supplies? Canvas Collectibles offers a variety of storage containers. They even have a holder with over 60 small compartments that hangs over a door and can store all your paint bottles. See *www.canvascollectibles.com*.

BUTTON THEME HAT

(extra quick and easy)

Sondra Says:

"It's amazing how many different types of buttons you can buy. I get mine in a package with 8 to 10 buttons in great shapes and designs."

Official Supply List

Fabric glue (available in craft or fabric stores)

Assortment of "novelty" buttons, shaped like sports equipment, flowers, animals, etc.

Plain-colored cloth hat

Ready . . . Set . . . Create!

1. It can't get much easier than this! Simply glue the buttons all over the hat and brim.
2. Let the glue dry and wear your designer hat.

A tip from Sondra:
If you don't have fabric glue, you can always use a needle and thread to sew the buttons on your hat.

Wash it out! Washaway paint for clothes lets you paint on shirts or cloth items. After you get tired of the design, wash the item and start over. The paint easily washes out. See *www.go-inkblots.com*.

VERY STRETCHY VISOR

Sondra Says:

"You'll like wearing this visor because it really stretches to fit comfortably on your head."

Official Supply List

Pencil

Paper

Scissors (pinking shears or scalloped-edged scissors are also fine)

One 9-by-12-inch sheet craft foam (any color)

Hole punch

Craft glue

Decorative items like sequins, craft foam scraps, buttons, markers, etc.

1 stretchy, coiled shoelace

Ready . . . Set . . . Create!

1. Trace the pattern on page 178 to a piece of paper.
2. Cut along the lines of the traced pattern.
3. Lay the paper pattern on your craft foam.
4. Lightly trace the shape onto the foam.
5. Cut out the shape. This is your visor.
6. Use a hole punch to make a hole on each end of the visor (punch holes at least ¼ inch from each end).
7. Get creative and glue an assortment of beads and craft foam to the visor, or use markers to decorate your visor.
8. Make sure the glue is dry.
9. String one end of the coiled shoelace into each hole.
10. You can easily adjust the coiled shoelace to custom-fit your head.

A tip from Sondra:
When you punch the holes, remember to punch them at least ¼ inch from each end so they don't tear.

Sometimes it's fun to get craft kits that come complete with all the supplies you need to make creative projects. Check out *www.craftsalacart.com* and look under the "kids ala cart" section.

JIFFY JEAN-SKIRT BAG

Sondra Says:

"This is a good way to keep on using the favorite jean skirt that you've outgrown."

Official Supply List

One jean skirt, with belt loops

Needle and thread *or* fabric glue

Sewing machine (optional)

Assortment of colorful buttons or "jewels"

Scarf, necktie, or wide ribbon at least 48 inches long

Ready . . . Set . . . Create!

1. Turn the skirt inside out and sew the bottom hem
   shut. (If you use a sewing machine, make sure an
   adult is with you.) You can also use fabric glue to seal
   the hem together.

2. Sew on the buttons you selected. If you have fake
   jewels, the fabric glue will attach them to the skirt
   permanently.

3. Weave the scarf or ribbon through the belt loops.
   When you gather this fabric, it closes your bag.

4. You can use the bag to store supplies for your favorite
   craft projects!

A tip from Sondra:
If you've never used fabric glue before, give it u
try. You'll be amazed how securely it binds buttons
and sequins to fabric.

Great American Crafts offers easy craft projects for the
whole family. Look for it on a newsstand or order it from
www.krause.com.

SUPER SPLATTER HAT

Sondra Says:

"I had so much fun doing this project that I used the splatter technique to decorate my dad's underwear!"

Official Supply List

Newspaper

One solid-colored cloth hat

3 to 4 colors of fabric paint

3 to 4 small yogurt containers or paper cups

Water

Plastic spoon

Old toothbrush or paintbrush

Silk flower (optional)

Ready . . . Set . . . Create!

1. Spread newspaper on your work surface. It's best to do this project outside.
2. Place the hat in the center of the paper.
3. Pour about 1 teaspoon paint in each empty container.
4. Add about 1 teaspoon water to each container of paint.
5. Mix the paint and water with the plastic spoon.
6. Dip the brush into one color of paint.
7. With a flick of your wrist, let the paint splatter on the hat. (You might want to practice "flicking" the paint on newspaper before you try your shirt.)
8. Repeat several times.
9. Rinse out the brush and repeat the process with the other colors.
10. If you want, attach a bright-colored silk flower to the front of your hat.
11. Let the hat dry thoroughly before wearing.

A tip from Sondra:
This hat looks extra cute if some of your fabric paint is labeled "shimmer." Shimmer paint shines when it dries.

Glue sticks, beads, and paint are listed in a free catalog from Wood-n-Crafts. Have an adult call them for you at (800) 444-8075.

BACKPACK KEY CHAINS

Sondra Says:

"Try making several of these to trade with your friends."

Official Supply List

Scissors (can use ones with decorative edges if you want)

1 sheet Shrink-It plastic (available in most craft stores)

Colored pencils and/or permanent markers

Hole punch

Cookie sheet

Oven

Key ring

Ready . . . Set . . . Create!

1. Cut plastic into a piece about 4 by 5 inches.

2. Make a design or picture on the plastic using the colored pencils or permanent markers. Try to add lots of details. When the pattern shrinks, it makes the picture look very intricate.

3. Cut around your design in whatever shape you want.

4. Use the paper punch to punch a hole *before* the plastic shrinks.

5. Place the plastic on a cookie sheet and have an adult shrink the plastic in the oven, following the package directions.

6. After the plastic is removed from the oven and is cool enough to handle, slip the key ring through the hole.

7. Make several of these and attach them to your backpack.

A tip from Sondra:
You'll get a colorful design by combining colored pencils and markers for each design.

Even if you are not a Girl Scout, you can still enjoy all the craft projects on their Web site: *www.gsusa.org*. They also offer tips on skits, games, and camping activities.

BABY'S HOMEMADE BIB

Sondra Says:

"Parents are very impressed if you make one of these bibs while baby-sitting their child!"

Official Supply List

Scissors (pinking shears, if possible)

Child's sweatshirt (find one that a preschooler has outgrown, or get one at a thrift shop)

Craft glue

2 small pieces of sponge

2 empty film canisters

Newspaper

2 colors of fabric paint

2 paper plates

Ready . . . Set . . . Create!

1. Prepare these three steps ahead of time if you plan on having a toddler "help."

2. Cut the sleeves and lower front and back off a sweatshirt.*

3. Glue two pieces of sponge on the bottom of the film canisters. These will be your stamps for chubby little hands to use. Let glue dry.

4. When you are with the young child, spread newspaper on your working surface. (It's also good idea to put an old paint smock on the child.)

5 Pour a small amount of paint on the paper plate.

6. Show the toddler how to hold on to the film canister and dip the sponge end in the paint.

7. Help the child dab the painted sponge on to the spread-out bib and stamp as many shapes as he or she wants. (Don't worry if the little one just wants to stamp over and over again.)

8. When the masterpiece is completed, place it somewhere out of reach to dry.

9. After it dries, your young artist can proudly drool on his or her one-of-a-kind bib!

*See the diagram on page 179 for help cutting your sweatshirt.

A tip from Sondra:
To make this bib as a gift for a young child, make intricate stamp designs and write the child's name with fabric paint.

A book with bright colorful craft ideas is Mary Engelbreit's *Hey Kids! Come Craft with Me* (Meredith Books). You'll find easy directions and illustrations.

FLEXIBLE TIARA

Sondra Says:

"Once you get the idea how to cover the pipe cleaners with beads, you can get creative and add more and more layers to your tiara."

Official Supply List

5 to 6 12-inch pipe cleaners

At least 150 pony beads, any two colors

Scissors

Hot glue (optional)

"Diamonds" (optional)

Ready . . . Set . . . Create!

1. Twist two pipe cleaners together so they make one long piece.

2. String pony beads over the entire pipe cleaner, leaving about 1 inch at both ends. This is the base for your tiara. You'll use about 75 beads.

3. When the pipe cleaner is covered with beads, twist the two ends together in a circle.

4. Using another color of bead, string them over a 12-inch pipe cleaner.

5. When the pipe cleaner is covered with beads, find the middle.

6. Take the middle section and wrap it once around the middle of your tiara base.

7. Make two loops and twist each end to the tiara base, about 14 beads out, on each side. You just finished the second layer of your tiara.

8. Cut a pipe cleaner 6 inches long.

9. Slip beads over this piece, which forms the top "arch" of your tiara. Connect it as shown in the diagram.

10. If you want, cut other pieces of pipe cleaner, cover with beads, and add more layers or designs.

11. Glue on a fake diamond or sparkling jewel before you wear your priceless tiara.

A tip from Sondra:
Feel free to be creative. String beads over the pipe cleaners and then just keep attaching them to create an elaborate tiara.

Most newsstands carry *Girl's Life* magazine. They offer articles about decorating your clothes and general craft projects. You can also visit their Web site: *www.girlslife.com.*

Chapter Two

Jazzy Jewelry

BAD HAIR DAY PIN

Sondra Says:

"Wear this pin to let your friends know you're trying to have a good attitude about your bad hair day!"

Official Supply List

Newspaper
Plaster of paris
Empty yogurt (or other similar) container to mix the plaster
Water
2 to 3 plastic spoons
2 to 3 jewelry pin backs or safety pins
Plastic wiggle eyes (optional)
Permanent markers or paint
Paintbrush, if using paint
About 10 inches of yarn
Scissors
Glue

Ready . . . Set . . . Create!

1. Cover your work surface with newspaper.
2. Pour about ½ cup of plaster of paris into the empty container.

3. Slowly add about ¼ cup water.

4. Stir until the plaster is like thick pudding. If it is too thick, add a few additional drops of water.

5. Lay the spoons on the newspaper. Wad up a small ball of excess newspaper and place it under the spoon handle. This levels out the "bowl" portion of the spoon.

6. Pour the plaster into the bowl of the spoons.

7. Gently place a pin back or safety pin in the wet plaster in each spoon.

8. Let them dry overnight.

9. The next day, "pop" the oval shapes out of the spoons. These are a perfect shape for your "face."

10. Decorate with wiggle eyes.

11. Use markers or paint to make cheeks, mouth, etc.

12. Cut the yarn into 5 pieces, each about 2 inches long.

13. Unravel each piece of yarn into 3 to 4 strands. This will make a frizzy, wild hairdo for your pins.

14. Apply glue to the back of each face. Glue the yarn hair around the face. Trim it if you want.

A tip from Sondra:
Never pour plaster of paris down the sink drain. Let it harden in the container and then put it in the garbage.

Sondra asked Art Linkletter, original host of the television show *Kids Say the Darndest Things,* what craft he enjoyed doing as a child. He said, "I grew up in San Diego where Charles Lindbergh and other aviation pioneers worked. I liked assembling model airplanes."

TWISTY TURNING STRAW NECKLACE

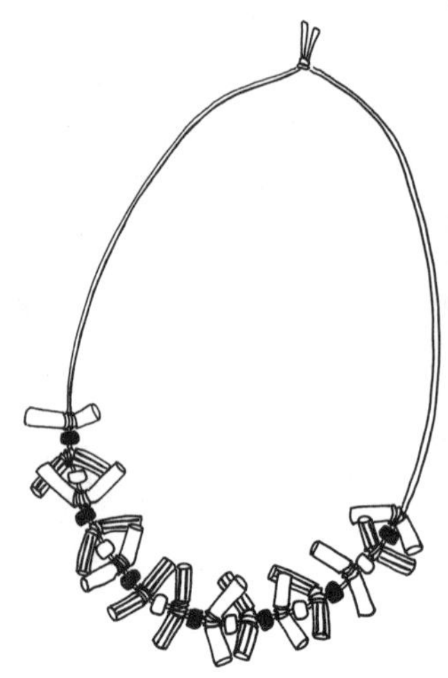

Sondra Says:

"This colorful necklace is great when you're playing dress up and want something bright and colorful."

Official Supply List

Embroidery floss

Needle with a large eye

15 to 20 pony beads

15 to 20 colored plastic straws with the bendable joint

Scissors

Ready . . . Set . . . Create!

1. Cut a section of embroidery floss about 24 inches long.

2. Thread the needle with the floss.

3. Put the ends of the floss together to make sure the finished necklace will fit over your head.

4. Tie a bead at one end of the floss so the other beads don't slide off.

5. Hold the straw in the center of the ridged (bendable) section. Cut the straw 1 inch from each side of the ridged section.

6. Cut all the straws in the same way.

7. Use the needle to poke through the center of your flexible "beads" and string the straw pieces on the floss.

8. Alternate the design with one round bead, a straw, a bead, etc.

9. When you have finished stringing your necklace, tie the two ends of the floss together.

10. Give your necklace an interesting design by bending each straw bead into a "U" shape in alternating directions.

A tip from Sondra:

Be careful when you poke the needle through the straw. You don't want to poke your finger instead of the straw!

You can buy bags of beads and necklace supplies from Fun Express. Ask an adult to call (800) 228-0122 for a free catalog.

ANIMAL CRACKER JEWELRY

Sondra Says:

"This craft project is great because you can eat the broken crackers while you're working!"

Official Supply List

Plain, unfrosted animal crackers

Clear nail polish or decoupage solution

Craft glue

Plain, smooth hair clip or headband

Pin backs, if you want to make pins

Ready . . . Set . . . Create!

1. Select 2 to 3 animal crackers and paint them with clear nail polish or the decoupage solution.
2. Let them dry. They will get shiny.
3. Glue the crackers on the headband or hair clip, or if you are making a pin, glue the cracker on the pin back.

A tip from Sondra:

If you want "fancier" animal crackers, use toothpicks or a small paintbrush to paint the fur, eyes, and other features on each animal. Add tiny wiggle eyes if you want. Cover with nail polish or decoupage solution.

Jo-Ann craft stores offer a wide assortment of reasonably priced craft items. Check out over 25 craft projects on their Web site at *www.joann.com.*

FUNNY FACE PINS

Sondra Says:

"These clown pins always turn out different, depending on the color and size of the buttons you use."

Official Supply List

Assortment of buttons (some should be two-hole buttons)

Popsicle sticks (one for each pin you make)

Glue

Fine-tip permanent markers

Felt or foam scraps

Scissors

Pin backs (one for each pin you make)

Ready . . . Set . . . Create!

1. Select three buttons. One will be the head of your clown and should have two holes in it. The other two buttons form the clown's body.

2. Lay the buttons upside down, in a line, one above the other. Make sure the top button is placed so the holes are side by side horizontally for eyes.

3. Ask an adult to cut or break a Popsicle stick so it fits the length of the three buttons without sticking over the edges. This acts as a support for your pin.

4. Spread glue on the stick and lay it on the three buttons.

5. Repeat the above steps for each pin you are making.

6. Let your pins dry.

7. Turn the buttons over and decorate your clowns with markers.

8. Use the scraps of foam or felt to make funny hats or clown collars. Cut the foam or felt if you need to.

9. Glue a pin back to the back of each pin.

A tip from Sondra:
Most craft stores sell packages of pin backs with double-backed adhesive. You just remove a protective piece of paper and stick the pin back wherever you need it.

> Like clowns? Look up a fun Web site at *www.funology.com*. It helps you learn magic, juggling, and crazy games.

FOURTH OF JULY NECKLACE

Sondra Says:

"Even though it will take longer, make sure each color of paint dries before you apply another color. That will give you a brighter design."

Official Supply List

18 to 21 small wooden thread spools (available in various sizes at craft stores)

Red, white, and blue acrylic paint or markers

Small paintbrush

Scotch tape

Thin ribbon or embroidery floss, about 18 inches long

8 red beads, 8 blue beads, and 8 white beads

Ready . . . Set . . . Create!

1. Divide the spools into 3 equal piles.

2. Paint the middle part of the spools in one pile blue, paint the middle part of the spools in another pile red, and paint the middle of the spools in the other pile white.

3. Let the spools dry.

4. Using paint or markers, decorate the tops and rims of the spools with contrasting red, white, or blue paint.

5. Let the paint dry.

6. Add any designs you like. An easy way to make polka dots is to simply dip the plastic end of a paintbrush in paint. Use this method to make tiny dots.

7. While the paint is drying, wrap a small piece of tape tightly around one end of the ribbon or embroidery floss. This makes a "needle" so you can string your spools.

8. Tie a knot at the other end of the ribbon. You don't want your spools to slip off!

9. String the spools, alternating them with red, white, and blue beads.

10. When all the spools and beads are used, tie the end and wear your Fourth of July necklace.

A tip from Sondra:
If you can't find small wooden spools at a craft store, try painting wooden beads in red, white, and blue. Or, make this necklace in your favorite colors so you can wear it any time of the year.

Walnut Hollow is the world's largest woodcraft manufacturer. It carries all shapes and sizes of wooden spools, unpainted doll furniture, and wood shapes. Visit their Web site at *www.walnuthollow.com*.

FANCY FOAM EARRINGS

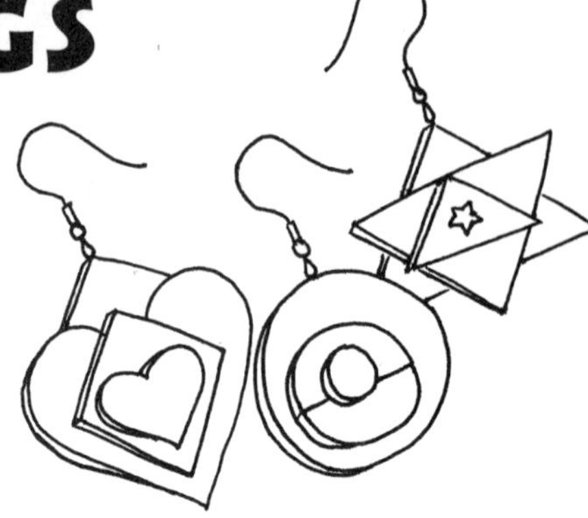

Sondra Says:

"These earrings are great if you like wild, modern art designs. If you don't have pierced ears, just glue these earrings to clip-on earring backs."

Official Supply List

Scissors

Lightweight craft foam (can be purchased in precut shapes or you can cut your own)

Toothpicks

Glue

Sequins (optional)

Earring hooks (for pierced ears) or clip-on earring backs

Ready . . . Set . . . Create!

1. Cut out a variety of small shapes from the foam if you don't have precut pieces. Any type of circle, heart, or strips will work.

2. Mix and match the shapes until you get a design you like. Even if you have precut pieces, you can cut them in half to make unique designs.

3. Use a toothpick to apply glue and attach the pieces together. Try layering different shapes on top of each other.

4. Glue on sequins if you want.

5. Let the pieces dry.

6. Glue on earring hooks or clip-on backs.

A tip from Sondra:
Squeeze a small amount of glue on a piece of scrap paper. Let it set for 5 to 10 minutes. It will get thick and sticky, which holds the foam pieces together better.

You can get foam scraps from Crafty Productions. Have an adult call them at (800) 925-6838 and order them for you. Have fun making soft and squishy crafts.

SHRINKING GHOST NECKLACE

Sondra Says:

"Shrinking these meat trays is fun. I do it all year-round and then use the shrunken trays as name tags or as part of a wind chime."

Official Supply List

Scissors
2 to 3 white Styrofoam meat trays
Black permanent markers
Hole punch
Cookie sheet
Oven
Black embroidery floss, about 24 inches long
Needle with large eye
About 20 orange beads

Ready . . . Set . . . Create!

1. Cut 4 to 5 free-form ghost shapes out of the meat tray. Each should be at least 5 inches tall.*
2. Outline the edges of the ghosts with black marker.
3. Draw spooky faces on the ghosts.

4. Punch 2 holes, side by side, in the top part of the head on each ghost. (These two holes help the necklace lay flat when you string the floss through.)

5. Place the Styrofoam ghosts on a cookie sheet.

6. Ask an adult to put the cookie sheet in an oven preheated to 300 degrees F.

7. The ghosts will shrink and get hard in about 60 to 90 seconds. Don't worry if they curl up at first. They should uncurl and lay flat after a few seconds.

8. Have an adult remove the cookie sheet from the oven and place the ghosts on the counter to cool.

9. Tie a big knot in one end of the embroidery floss.

10. Hold the ends of the embroidery floss together to make sure the finished necklace will fit over your head.

11. Thread the needle with the floss and string 2 orange beads, a ghost, 2 orange beads, etc.

12. When you run out of ghosts and beads, tie the ends together to complete your necklace.

*If you need help making ghosts, use the variety of patterns on pages 180 and 181.

A tip from Sondra:
Meat trays can have germs on them. Be sure to ask an adult to clean the trays with a soap and bleach solution before you use them.

Here's what Amy Grant, a popular singer, told Sondra about her favorite craft: "When I was little, I liked making fishing nets from coat hangers and panty hose. Then we'd catch fish in our creek."

BALLOON BUDDY

Sondra Says:

"It's a strange feeling to put stuffing inside a balloon, but the end result is a cute mouse pin."

Official Supply List

Heart-shaped balloon (available from most party or craft stores; any size works fine)

Cotton or batting

Pencil

Scrap ribbon

Needle

Black thread

Small black bead

Scissors

Glue

Wiggle eyes

Scrap pieces of pink felt

Black permanent marker

Pin back

Ready . . . Set . . . Create!

1. Stuff the heart-shaped balloon with the batting or cotton. A pencil can help you poke the filling inside. The top of the heart will form your mouse's ears.

2. Tie the scrap ribbon around the "neck" of your mouse. This keeps the stuffing inside.

3. Thread the needle with the black thread.

4. Sew on the black bead in the center of the balloon. Tie a knot so the thread is firmly attached to the bead. This is the mouse's nose.

5. Cut the thread so about 2 inches are loose on each side of the bead. This forms the whiskers.

6. Glue on the wiggle eyes, and scraps of pink felt for the ears.

7. Draw a small mouth with the permanent marker.

8. Glue a pin back to the back side of your stuffed mouse.

A tip from Sondra:
An adult may need to help you sew on the nose bead. It's sometimes difficult to get a needle to go through the balloon.

Ask an adult to take you to garage sales on a Saturday morning. You'll probably be able to buy inexpensive T-shirts to decorate, fancy buttons, and other craft items.

MINI-SLINKY NECKLACE

(extra quick and easy)

Sondra Says:

"It's fun to hear the strange popping sound that happens when you stretch the straw out to make the beads."

Official Supply List

Embroidery floss, about 24 inches

Blunt sewing needle or tape

15 to 20 assorted color straws with flexible "joints"

Scissors

15 to 20 assorted beads with wide holes, such as pony beads

Ready . . . Set . . . Create!

1. Tightly wrap a small piece of tape around one end of the embroidery floss to make a "needle." Or use a blunt sewing needle.

2. Put the ends of the embroidery floss together to make sure the finished necklace will fit over your head.

3. Hold a straw by each of its ends and pull. You want to stretch the "slinky" part of the straw. It sounds funny!

4. Cut the straw at each end of the joint you just stretched out.

5. Repeat this with different-colored straws until you have 15 to 20 slinky straw beads.

6. String one bead on the embroidery floss. Tie the end so the other beads don't slip off.

7. Make a pattern of straw beads and regular beads. Experiment with different combinations such as two straw beads, one regular bead, two straw beads, etc.

8. When you finish your necklace, tie the two ends of embroidery floss together.

A tip from Sondra:
To avoid wasting the rest of the straw, you can cut the straight straw sections into smaller pieces and use those for beads also.

Look up Grace Publications at *www.gracepublications.com* for a listing of great craft books, including *Pony Bead Playtime*, by Mary Ayers.

SWIRLED EARRINGS

Sondra Says:

"Remember when you finger-painted in preschool? This grown-up version of finger painting creates a swirled design."

Official Supply List

Scissors (with scalloped or designed edges if you have them)

Watercolor paper

Water

Paper towel

Tape

Scrap cardboard

Watercolors

Paintbrush

Glue

Clear nail polish

Tiny beads and sequins (optional)

Earring hooks (for pierced ears) or clip-on earring backs

Ready . . . Set . . . Create!

1. Cut a piece of watercolor paper into about 8½ inches by 5½ inches.

2. Wet the paper by dipping your finger in the water, and blot off excess water with paper towel.

3. Tape the paper to a piece of scrap cardboard or other hard surface. This stops the paper from curling as it dries.

4. Pick one color of watercolor paint and paint a random design on the wet paper.

5. Rinse the paintbrush.

6. Make another design with a different color, so the two colors are swirled (swirl with your fingers if you want).

7. Let the paper dry.

8. Find a section of the paper that has a nice pattern of blended colors, and cut it into two circles, hearts, or other shape, in whatever size you want the earring to be.

9. Cut 2 more shapes the same size. These will be on the back of your earring, so the pattern doesn't have to be perfect.

10. For each earring, glue the two shapes together, painted side out.

11. Coat the earrings with clear nail polish for a shine.

12. If you want, glue on tiny beads and/or sequins.

13. Glue on earring hooks or clip-on backs.

A tip from Sondra:
For best results use watercolor paper or heavy-duty linen paper.

Add interest to any type of paper cutting by using Fiskars scissors that cut scallops, zigzags, and loops. See *www.fiskars.com.*

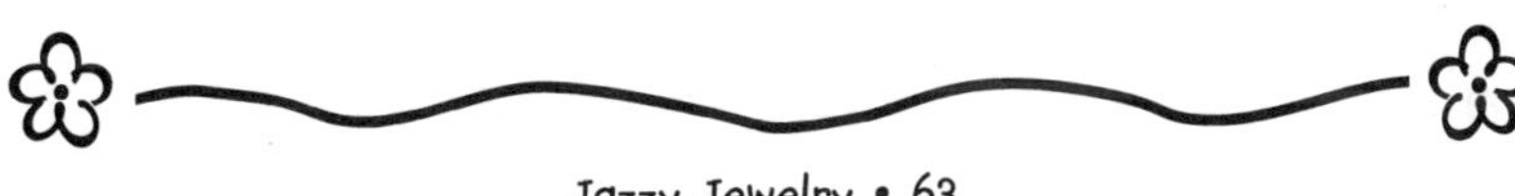

TWISTED JEWELRY

Sondra Says:

"I like making these because every piece of wire turns into a different 'bead,' depending on how you shape it."

Official Supply List

Thin, colored wire (available at most craft stores)

Thin dowel (thinner than a pencil)

Old scissors or wire cutters

6 to 10 assorted beads (optional)

Ready . . . Set . . . Create!

1. Take a piece of wire and twist one end so it has a 1-inch loop.

2. Cut the wire to your preferred length (you'll need about 12 inches of wire if you are making a choker, and about 6 inches if you make a bracelet).

3. Bend the loop to form a hook. This also stops the beads from slipping off the wire as you make your jewelry.

4. Select another piece of wire, about 12 inches long.

5. Tightly wrap this wire around the thin dowel.

6. When you've wrapped the entire wire, gently slip it off the dowel. There's your first bead!

7. Experiment with twisting the wire. Twist the wire back and forth and in and out so it looks like extra-curly hair.

8. Make 6 to 10 wire beads, depending on if you are making a choker or a bracelet.

9. String the wire beads over your straight wire with the hook. If you want, string a purchased bead between each wire bead.

10. When you have enough beads, make another 1-inch loop at the end of the stringing wire. Slip the hooked end into the loop to make a fastener for your piece of jewelry.

A tip from Sondra:
If you don't have a thin dowel, use the small straw that comes with a juice pack. If you wrap the wire around a Popsicle stick, you'll end up with a totally different-shaped bead.

If you like working with wire, check out the Web site *www.wirearts.com* for complete kits to make hair clips, wire people, etc.

FROSTY THE SNOWMAN PIN

Sondra Says:

"You can wear this snowman pin on December 21, the first day of winter."

Official Supply List

White paint

Small straw hat, about 2 inches in diameter

Blue paint

Small paintbrush

Glue

2 small wiggle eyes

1 tiny orange bead for the nose (If you don't have an orange bead, simply make a nose with an orange marker.)

Black permanent marker

Red and green yarn or embroidery floss

Scissors

Scrap of black felt or paper

Piece of cardboard, slightly bigger than the hat

Pin back

Ready . . . Set . . . Create!

1. Paint the top "bowl" part of the hat white to make your snowman's face. (Don't paint the brim.)
2. Let the paint dry.
3. Paint ¾ of the brim blue to make the sky behind the snowman.
4. Paint the remaining ¼ of the brim white. This forms the shoulders of your snowman.
5. Glue the wiggle eyes and nose on the white "face."
6. Use the black marker to draw a mouth.
7. Braid the floss or yarn to make a scarf and glue it around the snowman's "neck."
8. Cut out a hat from the black felt or paper and glue it on the snowman's head.
9. Dip the hard plastic end of your paintbrush in the white paint. Use it to make dots for snow on the blue "sky" portion of the straw hat.
10. Trace the entire hat on a piece of cardboard. Cut out the circle.
11. Glue the cardboard on the back of the hat. Let it dry.
12. Glue a pin back to the cardboard.

A tip from Sondra:
A pin back with self-adhesive sticks to the cardboard better.

Delta Paints offers gloss finishes
that will make your snowman shiny. Check craft stores
or try *www.deltacrafts.com*.

CRAZY CARROT FOSSIL NECKLACE

Sondra Says:

"It sounds crazy to dry carrots to create jewelry, but you'll be surprised how carrot slices turn into beads that look like ancient fossils. Maybe this is what baby dinosaur teeth look like."

Official Supply List

2 carrots (peel one carrot)

Cutting board

Sharp knife

24 inches of embroidery floss

Needle with a large eye

Assortment of pony beads; shiny ones give the best results

Ready . . . Set . . . Create!

1. Have an adult with you as you cut the carrots on the cutting board into ¼-inch-thick slices.

2. After you have 15 to 20 slices, cut a few of the larger pieces in half to give you a variety of sizes.

3. Thread the needle with embroidery floss, and poke a hole in the middle of each carrot slice. Wiggle the needle to enlarge the hole. It works best to place the

carrot slice on the cutting board and poke the needle
in the middle.

4. Put the ends of the embroidery floss together to make
   sure the finished necklace will fit over your head.

5. String the carrot slices on the floss.

6. When you have all the pieces strung, lay your necklace
   near a heating vent. If you live in a warm climate,
   place the carrot slices in the sun.

7. A couple of times a day, slide the carrot pieces back
   and forth on the floss. This keeps the hole from drying
   directly to the floss.

8. After 2 to 3 days, your beads should be hard, pale
   orange, and crinkly. You've made crazy carrot beads!

9. Remove the beads from the floss. Select which beads
   you like and restring them on the floss, alternating
   with pony beads if you want.

10. Tie the ends of the floss when you are finished.

11. Wear your necklace and see if people can guess what
    your special beads are made from!

A tip from Sondra:
Experiment with peeled and unpeeled carrots. You'll
get a different colored bead if you leave the skin on.

SKD Crafts offers a colorful catalog with beads, feathers,
confetti, and rhinestones. Ask an adult to get the catalog
for you by calling (800) I-LUV-SKD.

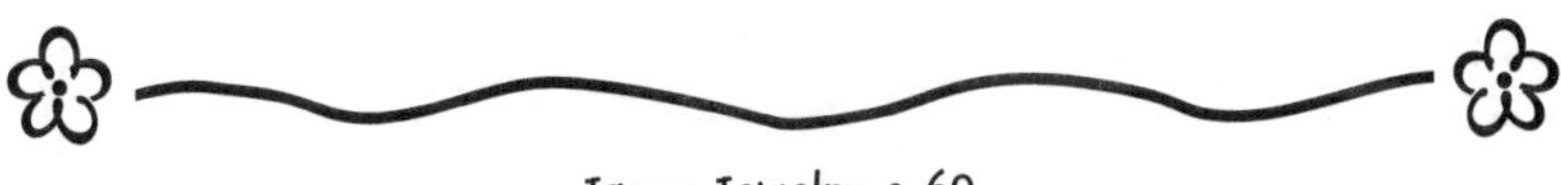

HOT GLUE JEWELRY

Sondra Says:

"Colored glue sticks let you make all sorts of bright jewelry pieces. Just make sure an adult helps you use the glue gun."

Official Supply List

Black permanent marker

Paper

Clear piece of plastic, such as an empty CD case (it can be reused)

2 to 3 glue guns (Craft stores sell these for under $2.00 each and they can be used for many craft projects.)

Colored hot glue stick pellets (available at any craft store)

Clip-on earring backs or pin backs

Ready . . . Set . . . Create!

1. Use the black marker to draw a simple shape on the paper, such as a heart or circle. It should be the size of an earring or small pin.

2. Place the picture under the empty CD case so you can easily see the design.

3. With an adult close by, heat the glue gun and insert a stick of colored glue.

4. Using the picture as a pattern, squeeze the colored glue directly on the plastic CD cover.

5. When the shape is filled in, let the glue dry.

6. Peel the cooled glue shape off the plastic. This is the base for your jewelry.

7. Be creative and add small dots of glue in another color, or make a smaller shape and glue the two pieces together. You can use your colored glue sticks to attach several pieces to each other.

8. Glue the pieces on clip-on earring backs or pin backs.

A tip from Sondra:
You'll want to practice several times to get the right amount of pressure to fill in your designs. If you only have one glue gun, ask an adult to cut a glue stick in half. Then when you run out of that color, simply insert a stick from another color.

Have an adult contact Gloobie at (888) 456-6243 for a free catalog of craft projects you can make with colored glue sticks.

QUICK-ZIP FRIENDSHIP BRACELETS

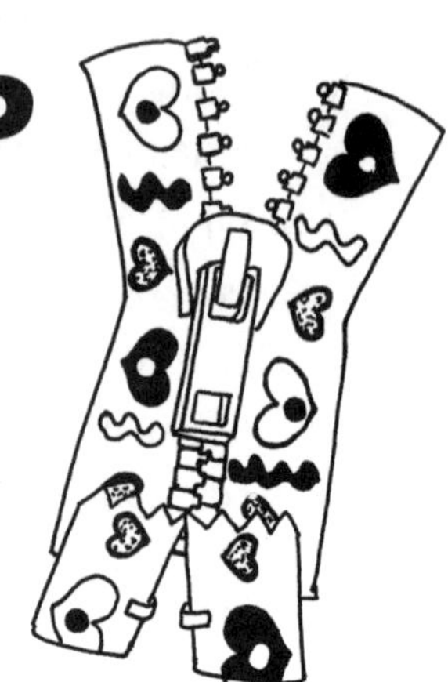

Sondra Says:

"These are fun to make with a friend. When you finish decorating the zipper, separate the two pieces so you each get to wear half the bracelet."

Official Supply List

One 7-inch *separating* heavy-duty zipper with plastic teeth

2 inches of Velcro cut into four ½-inch sections

Needle and thread

Fabric paints or permanent markers

Small paintbrushes if using fabric paint

Toothpicks (optional)

Ready . . . Set . . . Create!

1. Unzip and separate the two halves of the zipper.
2. On one end of the zipper half, sew a 1-by-½-inch square of Velcro.

3. Turn the zipper over and wrap it around your wrist. Try to figure out where the second piece of Velcro needs to go so the bracelet stays on your wrist. The two Velcro pieces will be your fastening.

4. Using the needle and thread, sew on the other square of Velcro.

5. Sew the two pieces of Velcro on the other half of the zipper also.

6. Lay each piece of the zipper on a flat surface.

7. Decorate the zipper with the markers or fabric paint. Because the zipper has a rough texture, you might find it easier to "paint" with toothpicks instead of a paintbrush.

8. Let the paint dry. It's fun for you and your friend to each decorate one half of the zipper. Then exchange pieces as a true sign of friendship.

A tip from Sondra:
Velcro is also available with double-backed adhesive. Then you can just stick it on the zipper and you don't have to sew it on.

Most kids use inexpensive paintbrushes. You'll get better results by using good quality brushes. Next time you have a birthday, ask for a few brushes from a company such as Loew-Cornell. See *www.loew-cornell.com.*

HARVEST NECKLACE

Sondra Says:

"These beads will still turn out looking fine, even if you have trouble rolling them into a ball."

Official Supply List

2 rolls of polymer-type clay with a pattern
Sharp knife
Toothpicks
Cookie sheet
Oven
Needle with large eye
24 inches of embroidery floss
15 to 20 pony beads, contrasting with the colors in your clay

Ready . . . Set . . . Create!

1. Read the directions on the clay package about how to warm it. The clay will make better beads if it is warmed.

2. Slice the roll of warmed clay into ¼-inch sections.

3. Gently poke a toothpick into the center of each section of cut clay. Wiggle the toothpick back and forth to widen the hole.

4. Warm the other package of clay. Slice this roll into ½-inch sections.

5. Take each of these pieces and roll it into a ball.

6. Use the toothpick to make holes in these round beads.

7. Place all the flat and round pieces of clay on a cookie sheet.

8. Have an adult bake it in the oven according to package instructions.

9. After the beads are baked and cooled, thread the needle with the floss.

10. Put the ends of the floss together to make sure the finished necklace will fit over your head.

11. String the beads in whatever pattern you want. You could try one flat bead, one pony bead, one round bead, etc.

12. When all the beads are used up, tie the ends of the floss together.

13. Wear your necklace!

A tip from Sondra:

If you want to make your necklace extra special, use some clay to make one "different" bead as the center of your necklace. This could be a long rectangular bead or maybe a narrow cylindrical shape.

Most craft stores carry AMACO Millefiori Canes, which come in rolls complete with intricate clay designs. Their Web site, *www.amaco.com,* has additional craft projects.

TINY DROP EARRINGS

Sondra Says:

"Make these earrings when you have plenty of time. It takes patience to make the tiny paint drops."

Official Supply List

3-by-5-inch piece of plastic canvas, any color

Empty Styrofoam meat tray

Pencil

2 to 3 colors "puff" paint

Assortment of seed beads

Scissors

Wire earring loops or clip-on backings

Ready . . . Set . . . Create!

1. Lay the plastic canvas in the empty meat tray. This keeps your work area clean, because some paint will soak through the canvas holes.

2. Sketch out a shape on the plastic canvas with the pencil.

3. Draw the same-size shape next to the first design, so you have your pair of earrings.

4. Practice on a corner of the plastic canvas to squeeze the paint so a tiny drop fills in each plastic square. When you feel comfortable making even-sized drops of paint, start painting your earrings.

5. After all the squares are filled in, gently place a few beads on top of a few squares of paint. When the paint dries, the beads will stay in place.

6. Let the paint dry overnight.

7. When the paint is dry, cut along the pencil lines to form the shape of your earrings.

8. Slip a wire hook through each earring, or glue on a clip-on earring back to the plastic canvas.

9. Show off your teeny-tiny paint-drop earrings!

A tip from Sondra:
Sometimes, after the paint dries, one or two of the plastic canvas squares will have a paint gap. Just go ahead and reapply another drop of paint in the same color to fill in the space.

You've probably made key chains from plastic gimp at camp. Now Pepperell Braiding Company offers gimp that changes colors, glows in the dark, and is scented. Visit their Web site at *www.pepperell.com.*

Chapter Three

HAIR CARE WITH FLAIR

BUBBLE-BLOWING HAIR BOW

Sondra Says:

"Blowing colored bubbles on the handkerchief gives you a bright-colored design that looks great tied around your ponytail. You'll probably like blowing the bubbles so much you'll make several of these."

Official Supply List

Newspaper

2 to 3 empty tuna fish cans or similar-sized containers

1 small bottle bubble-blowing solution

2 to 3 different colors of acrylic paint

2 to 3 straws

White handkerchief (can be purchased at dollar stores)

Ready . . . Set . . . Create!

1. Lay out the newspaper to protect your work surface.
2. Fill each tuna can half full with the bubble solution.
3. Add 4 to 5 drops of each color paint to each container, so you have three different colors.
4. Stir each solution with a straw.
5. Choose one color and blow into the straw, until a mound of bubbles comes over the top of the can.
6. Lay a section of the handkerchief on top of the bubbles.
7. Lift up the handkerchief and admire your bubble design.
8. Repeat the process with the other colors.
9. Try layering one color of bubbles over another. What happens when you put yellow bubbles on top of a blue design?

A tip from Sondra:
To get an idea how this project works, practice by putting scrap paper on top of the bubble mounds first. If you don't have bubble solution, just add 2 to 3 teaspoons dishwashing soap to water and then add the paint. You'll still get your bubbles.

PERSONALIZED HAIR CLIPS

Sondra Says:

"I can never find barrettes or other personalized items with my name on them at stores. If you have an unusual name, you'll especially enjoy making these."

Official Supply List

Alphabet letter pasta

Scrap paper

Permanent markers

Narrow barrettes (as many as you want to personalize)

Tiny beads (optional)

Scrap ribbons (optional)

Toothpicks

Glue

Clear nail polish

Ready . . . Set . . . Create!

1. Sort through the pasta letters and find the letters in your name.

2. Lay the letters on a piece of scrap paper. This way you won't get ink on your work surface.

3. Use the permanent markers to color the letters.

4. If you want, use the permanent markers to also decorate the barrette. Glue on tiny beads or ribbons for an extra fancy clip.

5. Dab the toothpick in the glue and spread some on the center of the clip.

6. Place the letters on the glue to spell your name. Don't worry about the glue showing. It will dry clear.

7. Let dry.

8. To give a shiny finish to your name, coat with clear nail polish.

A tip from Sondra:
Use tweezers to place the letters on the glue. It makes it easier to handle the tiny pieces of pasta.

Can Do Crafts publishes a book called *Hair Beads and Bows,* which gives more ideas on how to make your own hair accessories. See *www.d-originals.com.*

SPARKLING FASHION BARRETTE

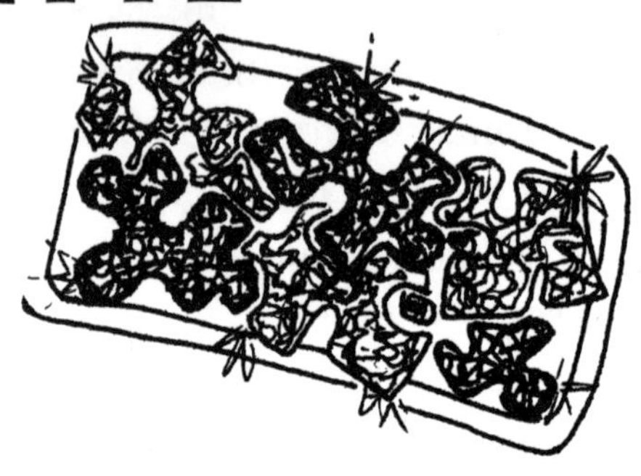

Sondra Says:

"With a little work, you can transform an ordinary barrette or headband into a glittery masterpiece."

Official Supply List

Glitter, two or more colors

Resealable plastic sandwich bags

Glue

10 to 12 puzzle pieces (smaller sizes work best, such as from a 500-piece puzzle)

Plain plastic or metal headband or barrette (available at most dollar stores)

Ready . . . Set . . . Create!

1. Put about 1 tablespoon of glitter in a resealable bag.
2. Spread glue on one side of 2 to 3 puzzle pieces.

3. Put the glued puzzle pieces in the bag and close it tightly.

4. Shake!

5. Remove the puzzle pieces and gently shake off any extra glitter.

6. Place the pieces, "unglittered" side down, on a flat surface.

7. Repeat with other puzzle pieces, until you have 5 to 6 pieces.

8. Repeat steps 1 through 7 with a different color of glitter, using new puzzle pieces.

9. Let your glittery puzzle pieces dry overnight.

10. Spread glue on the barrette or headband.

11. Glue on the puzzle pieces, overlapping them slightly.

12. Let dry.

13. Wear your hair accessory out in the sun and watch it sparkle.

A tip from Sondra:
Spray a light mist of hair spray on the puzzle pieces to help hold the glitter on.

Pay a visit to your local dollar store.
They often sell packages of 2 to 3 headbands for only $1.
You can decorate them in many ways.

BEADED STRETCHY HEADBAND

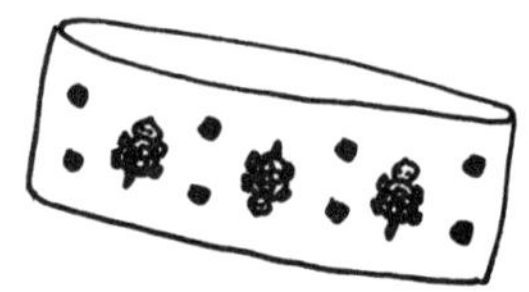

Sondra Says:

"This craft is a good way to practice learning how to sew by hand."

Official Supply List

Stretchy headband (cotton or a wool one you wear on cold
   days)
Book
Needle and thread
10 to 20 assorted beads
Scissors

Ready . . . Set . . . Create!

1. Stretch the headband over the book. This makes sewing easier.

2. Thread the needle and tie a knot in the end of the thread.

3. Select a bead and sew it on the headband.

4. After you sew on one bead, cut the thread and tie a knot.

5. Start over, sewing on another bead the same way. You can make designs with the beads, or just sew them on in a random pattern.

A tip from Sondra:
Because the headband stretches, sew on each bead with 4 to 5 "stitches" so it holds up to wear and tear.

Craftworks magazine has creative ideas
for adults and children. Look for it at craft stores or
www.craftworksmag.com.

STICKER HEADBAND

(extra quick and easy)

Sondra Says:

"These are fun to make as a craft project at birthday parties. All your friends will go home with different headbands."

Official Supply List

Assortment of stickers (if possible, get some stickers in the shape of letters)

Plain-colored plastic headband

Decoupage and brush (optional)

Ready . . . Set . . . Create!

1. If you have alphabet stickers, select the letters that make up your name.

2. Attach the stickers to the top center of the headband so they spell your name.

3. Add additional stickers on each side of your name.

4. To get a shiny finish, spread a layer of decoupage over the entire headband.

5. Let dry.

6. If you don't have decoupage, that's okay. Your headband is finished!

A tip from Sondra:

Can't find alphabet stickers? Just use a permanent marker to neatly print your name on the headband. Then add a small dot at the end of any letters with straight lines to give your letters a "fancier" look. Example:

Sondra

Check out Plaid Paint's Web site at *www.plaidonline.com.* You'll find ideas for painting fabrics as well as other craft projects.

POM-POM HEADBAND

(extra quick and easy)

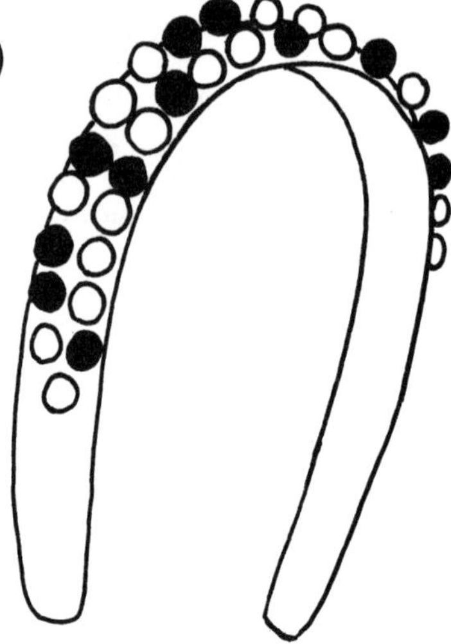

Sondra Says:

"If you want to snazz up your plain headbands, this is an easy way to add color and 'poof.'"

Official Supply List

Craft glue

Smooth, plain headband (cloth or plastic—doesn't matter as long as the headband is smooth)

20 to 30 ¼- or ½-inch pom-poms

Ready . . . Set . . . Create!

1. Spread craft glue on ⅓ of the headband. One at a time, place the pom-poms on the headband. You can make straight rows, or just put them on in a random pattern.
2. Spread the glue on the second third of the headband and repeat the process.
3. You guessed it! Just put glue on the rest of the headband and add pom-poms.
4. Let dry overnight.

A tip from Sondra:
For certain holidays, buy pom-poms in coordinating colors. You could use red and white for Valentine's Day or orange and black for Halloween.

Sometimes fuzzy pom-poms are difficult to glue.
Try a product such as Quick and Tacky from Delta.
It is thicker than regular glue and will keep pom-poms
from rolling away from you.

BAKED BARRETTES

Sondra Says:

"This is a good way to use up scraps of polymer clay, because you just need a small amount of clay to cover each hair barrette."

Official Supply List

Small amount of polymer clay (the kind you bake in the oven)

Rolling pin for crafts or any soup can

Plastic or metal barrettes (can be scratched or old)

Scissors

Assortment of beads or buttons

Fork or toothpick (optional)

Cookie sheet

Oven

Ready . . . Set . . . Create!

1. Roll the clay in your hands for a few minutes to get it soft and pliable.

2. Use the rolling pin or soup can to roll out the clay. Try to get it ¼ inch thick.

3. Drape the flattened clay over the hair barrette and gently press down. With scissors, trim any clay hanging over the edge. If you just have a small amount of extra clay, fold it under to the back side of the barrette. Repeat for each barrette you are "baking."

4. Firmly press beads or buttons in the clay. You can also make designs in the clay with the prongs of a fork or a toothpick.

5. When finished, put the barrettes on the cookie sheet.

6. Have an adult help you put the cookie sheet in the oven. Follow the clay package directions for temperature and time.

7. Even though you bake the clay at a low temperature, the cookie sheet will be hot. Make sure an adult removes it from the oven.

8. Let the barrettes cool before you wear them.

A tip from Sondra:
Be sure to wash your hands after working with any type of polymer clay.

For more ideas on working with different types of clay, check out Crayola's Web site at *www.crayola.com*. Their new Modeling Magic comes in bright colors and air-dries.

CRAWLING CATERPILLAR CLIP

Sondra Says:

"This is one type of bug you won't mind having crawl through your hair."

Official Supply List

Craft glue

Smooth hair clip (barrette), at least 3 inches long

4 or 5 fuzzy pom-poms, ½ inch (any color)

1¾-inch fuzzy pom-pom, a different color than smaller ones

Black pipe cleaner or embroidery floss

2 small wiggle eyes

Ready . . . Set . . . Create!

1. Spread the craft glue on top of the barrette in a straight line.
2. Let the glue dry 2 to 3 minutes. This makes it "stickier," and the pom-poms won't roll off.
3. Place the smaller pom-poms in a row to form the body of your caterpillar.
4. Before gluing on the larger pom-pom as the head, wrap the pipe cleaner or floss around it to form the antenna.
5. Place the larger pom-pom on one end of your caterpillar body to create the head.
6. Glue wiggle eyes on the head.
7. Let the glue dry before putting this cute creature in your hair.

A tip from Sondra:
Pom-poms are sometimes difficult to glue. It works best to press them gently on the glue and let them dry. Try not to shift their position once you set them down.

If you can't go to camp, look up Camp Craftopia at *www.craftopia.com.* This Web site has reasonably priced craft kits for kids of all ages.

RIBBON-WEAVING HAIR COMBS

Sondra Says:

"You can easily take ordinary hair combs and make them look extra special with just ribbons and beads."

Official Supply List

Scissors

⅛-inch ribbon (whatever color you like)

Plain hair combs

Tacky glue

Assortment of tiny beads or ribbon flowers

Ready . . . Set . . . Create!

1. Cut a piece of ribbon about 12 inches long.
2. Wrap one end of the ribbon around the first "tooth" of the hair comb on the underneath side.
3. Tie a knot at that end so the ribbon stays attached.
4. Wrap the ribbon in and out of each "tooth."
5. Try to keep the ribbon smooth and untwisted.
6. When you reach the end of the comb, simply begin wrapping the ribbon back the way you came. Make sure to criss-cross the ribbon.
7. When you get to the end, tie a small knot on the underside of the comb. Add a dab of tacky glue on the knot to keep it from unraveling. When the glue dries, trim off any extra ribbon.
8. Using your creativity, add any beads, buttons, or ribbon flowers on top of the woven ribbon section.

A tip from Sondra:
If you want a totally different design, use a different-colored ribbon when you criss-cross over the first woven section.

Find inexpensive ribbon and lace
on this Web site: *wwwcheeplace.com.*

SPARKLING STARBURST HEADBAND

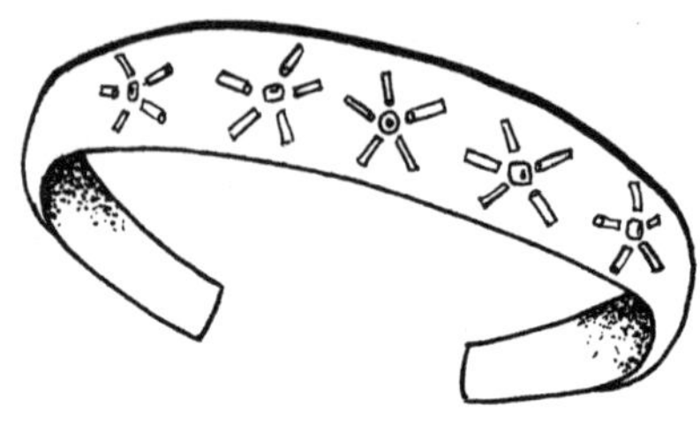

Sondra Says:

"Try to keep the glue off your fingers when decorating these headbands. Otherwise, you'll have tiny beads all over your fingertips!"

Official Supply List

Tacky glue

Scrap piece of cardboard for glue

1 cotton swab

Fabric headband (white works best to hide any dried glue)

5 to 7 small Indian seed beads, any color

25 to 30 bugle beads, ¼-inch, any color (they look like tiny tubes)

Ready . . . Set . . . Create!

1. Pour about one ½ teaspoon glue on the cardboard.
2. Dip the cotton swab in the glue.
3. Find the top center of the headband and use the cotton swab to spread the glue in a circle about the size of a dime.
4. Place a small seed bead in the center of the glue circle.
5. Add five bugle beads around the center bead, like the spokes on a wheel.
6. Repeat the process on both sides of your first "starburst" until you have five to seven completed. Don't worry about the circle of glue because it dries clear.
7. Let the glue dry before wearing the headband.

A tip from Sondra:
These beads are tiny and are sometimes hard to get in the correct position. Try using tweezers to put the beads where you want them.

If you are looking for a variety of craft projects, check out *www.makingfriends.com*. The directions are easy, plus each craft has a photograph so you can get an idea how the finished project looks.

FANCY FAIRY HEADBAND

Sondra Says:

"This 'fluttery' headband is fun to make if you are dressing up as a princess or fairy."

Official Supply List

Scissors

1 yard each of 3 colors of thin, sheer ribbon

Thin headband with extra long "prongs" that slide in your hair

Ready . . . Set . . . Create!

1. Cut the ribbon into 7-inch sections.

2. Simply tie a piece of ribbon in a knot between each prong of the headband.

3. When you have the headband covered with ribbon strips, decide whether you like the length of each ribbon. Trim the ribbon if you want a smaller headband.

4. If you want a more jagged look, cut each end of the ribbon into a "V" shape.

5. Get out your fairy wings and start fluttering!

A tip from Sondra:
To make your headband sparkle even more, slip a shiny bead over the ribbon as you tie the knot.

Want ideas for wearable art, recyclable crafts, or games? Look up *www.childfun.com* for hours of fun on the computer.

LACY, WAVY SCRUNCHIE

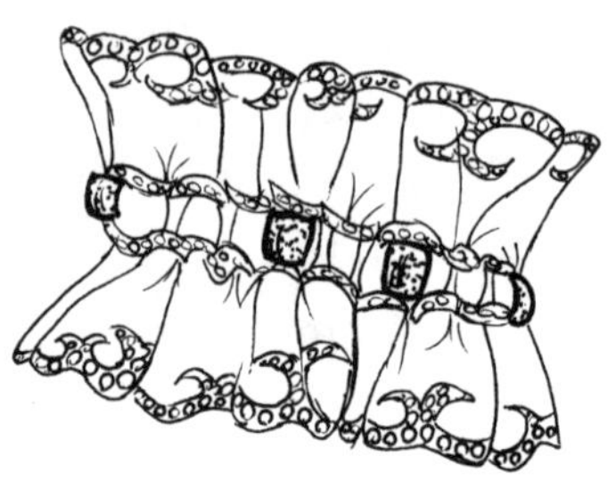

Sondra Says:

"You can make this in minutes with different colors of cotton lace."

Official Supply List

2 safety pins

10 to 12 inches of ⅛-inch elastic

Tape

About 24 inches of cotton lace, with evenly spaced holes along the edge or middle of the lace

Pony beads

Sewing needle and thread

Scissors (for cutting thread)

Ready . . . Set . . . Create!

1. Pin a safety pin on one end of the elastic.

2. On the other end, tightly wrap a small piece of tape. This forms a "needle" for you to push through the holes in the lace and the pony beads.

3. Starting with the taped end, weave in and out of the cotton lace.

4. Add a pony bead every three to four "holes" in the lace.

5. When you are about halfway through the lace, pin the opposite end of elastic to the end of the lace. You don't want to accidentally pull the elastic all the way through!

6. As you get to the end of the lace, remove the tape.

7. Use the needle and thread to sew the two ends of elastic firmly together.

8. Even out the lace and pull your hair back into a stylish ponytail.

A tip from Sondra:

If you don't want to sew the two ends of the elastic together, you can use one safety pin to join the ends. The lace will cover up the pin.

Get more "stretchy" ideas for hair accessories or jewelry from the book *Strictly Stretch Jewelry,* by Katie Hacker (Hot Off the Press).

BIG BEADED HEADBAND

Sondra Says:

"It's fun seeing how the headband is formed using marbles and beads."

Official Supply List

Scissors

One stretch fabric headband that is a "tube" (available at most dollar stores)

5 wooden beads with a hole at least ½ inch wide

Pencil

4 marbles or round beads the size of marbles

Needle and thread

Ready . . . Set . . . Create!

1. Cut the headband in half along the seam where it was stitched together.
2. Slip one wooden bead over the fabric and slide it to the center of the headband. Use the eraser end of the pencil to push the fabric through the bead. (Since this is the center bead, you might want to paint it a different color.)
3. Slip a marble *inside* the fabric on one side, so it is next to the center bead.
4. Slide another bead *over* the fabric until it reaches the marble.
5. Add one more marble inside and one bead outside the fabric.
6. Repeat this process with the other side of the headband.
7. Simply sew the two ends of the headband together and you have a new accessory for your hair.

A tip from Sondra:
If the headband seems too tight with the beads, sew a small piece of elastic to the two end pieces of fabric.

The Starline company sells a handy
Tote-It Carry All Bag for all your craft supplies.
Visit them at *www.starline.com.*

Chapter Four

Cool Clothes from Head to Toe

TIRE TRACK T-SHIRT

Sondra Says:

"Try and have your friends guess how you got the design on your shirt. They probably won't guess it is from tire tracks."

Official Supply List

Washed cotton T-shirt or sweatshirt

Scrap cardboard

Scissors

Contact paper (doesn't matter what color or pattern)

Fabric paint, 2 to 3 colors

Paper plates (one plate for each color of paint)

Small race track-type toy car (smaller wheels work best)

Permanent marker (optional)

Ready . . . Set . . . Create!

1. Lay the shirt on a smooth surface. Smooth out any wrinkles.
2. Slip a piece of cardboard inside the shirt so the paint doesn't soak through.
3. Cut a 12-inch-by-12-inch square of Contact paper. Don't peel it apart yet.

4. From the center of the contact paper square, cut out a basic shape such as a heart or square, 5 to 6 inches in diameter. Put aside. You won't be using the cut-out shape.

5. Gently peel off the backing from the paper with the shape cut out of it. With an adult's help, place the sticky paper on the shirt. Make sure the cut-out design is where you want the decoration to be.

6. Press the contact paper firmly to the shirt around the edges of the cut-out design. This is your homemade stencil.

7. Pour fabric paint on paper plates, one color per plate.

8. Here's the fun part. Place the wheels of the toy car in the paint. Move the car back and forth to get paint on the tires.

9. Take the car and "drive" it back and forth over the exposed part of shirt material inside the stencil.

10. Wash the car tires and repeat with another color until you get the design you want.

11. Let the paint dry overnight.

12. Peel off the sticky paper, and you'll have a unique tire track designed shirt. If you want, trace the outline of the stencil design with a permanent marker.

> Another book that gives ideas for decorating T-shirts is *T-Shirt Fun,* by Petra Boase (Lorenz Books).

EASY TIE-DYE TENNIS SHOES

Sondra Says:

"These shoes look great on Halloween if you want to dress up like a hippie. You'll be surprised at how easy this tie-dye project is."

Official Supply List

Newspaper

White cloth tennis shoes

Water

Small bowl or yogurt lid

Scraps of colored tissue paper (bright colors work best)

Ready . . . Set . . . Create!

1. Lay out the newspaper on a table.
2. Remove the laces from the shoes if you want solid-colored laces. Otherwise, leave them in to be tie-dyed also.
3. Put 1 to 2 teaspoons of water in the bowl or lid.
4. Crumple up one color of tissue paper to about the size of a walnut.
5. Lightly touch the tissue paper to the water.
6. Dab the tissue paper on the shoe in a random pattern. The color from the paper will "bleed." Repeat with 2 to 3 different colors, until you get the tie-dye look you want.

A tip from Sondra:
This project stains your fingers. If you want, wear rubber gloves or use a clothespin to pick up the wads of tissue.

Get more ideas on wearable art from *Better Homes & Gardens' Incredibly Awesome Crafts for Kids* magazine. It features fun crafts with step-by-step instructions.

FUZZY LADYBUG SHIRT

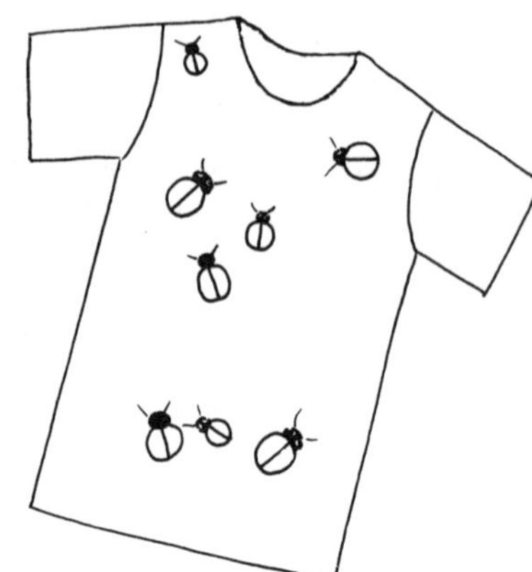

Sondra Says:

"Try making a whole family of ladybugs out of different-sized pom-poms."

Official Supply List

Light-colored T-shirt or sweatshirt

Scrap cardboard

2-inch or 2-½-inch red pom-poms (1 for every bug you plan to make)

Washable glue (available at most craft stores)

Needle with large eye

14- to 16-inch black embroidery floss

Scissors

½-inch black pom-pom (1 for every bug you plan to make)

Small wiggle eyes (optional)

Ready . . . Set . . . Create!

1. Decide where on the shirt you want the ladybug.

2. Insert a piece of cardboard inside the shirt at that location. That stops the glue from soaking through the material.

3. Dip half the large pom-pom into washable glue.

4. Place the pom-pom on the shirt, glue side down.

5. Thread the needle with the embroidery floss.

6. Pull the needle through the shirt from underneath, to come up right next to one side of the pom-pom.

7. Pull the thread over the top of the pom-pom, which makes the stripe down the back of your ladybug.

8. Bring the needle back through the material and tie a knot underneath.

9. Cut the embroidery floss.

10. Glue the small black pom-pom to form the ladybug's head.

11. Glue wiggle eyes on the head.

12. Glue scraps of embroidery floss on the head to make antennas.

13. Make as many ladybugs as you want to cover your shirt. If you want to change the size of your ladybugs, just change the size of your pom-poms.

A tip from Sondra:
When working with tiny objects such as wiggle eyes, use a toothpick to spread the glue. That way the tiny eyes won't stick to your fingers.

Have you ever seen fuzzy pom-poms with a hole in the middle? This new craft item comes from Aldastar Corporation. Have an adult call (973) 742-6787 for information, or check your local craft store.

GLOW-IN-THE-DARK PJS

Sondra Says:

"I have glow-in-the-dark stars on my ceiling. After making this shirt, I have matching glow-in-the-dark pajamas."

Official Supply List

Big dark blue or black T-shirt

Scrap cardboard

Sponges (precut star- and moon-shaped sponges or cut your own*)

Scissors

Glow-in-the-dark paint

Empty meat tray or other disposable container for paint

*To make it easier, use the star and moon patterns on pages 182 and 183.

Embossed Velvet Material Bag

Jean Pocket Purses

Harvest Necklace
Shrinking Ghost
Necklace
Fourth of July Necklace
Frosty the Snowman Pin
Baked Barrette 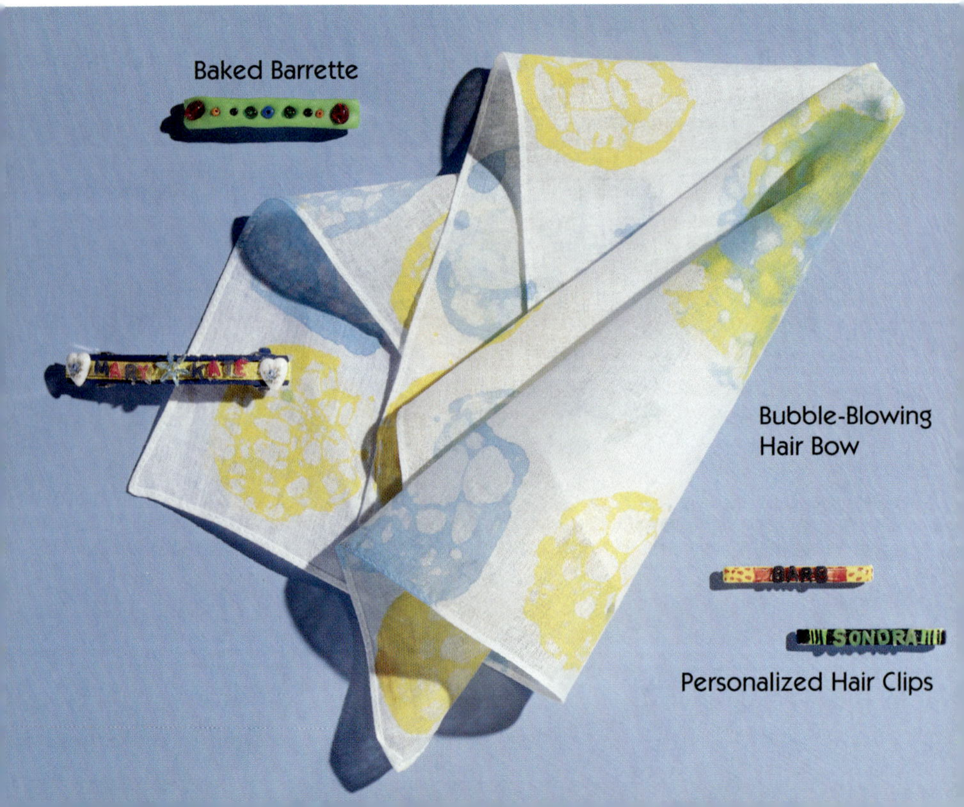
Bubble-Blowing
Hair Bow
Personalized Hair Clips

Flower Power Shoes
Baked
Ribbon
Delights
Fancy Shoelaces
Mini-Slinky Necklace 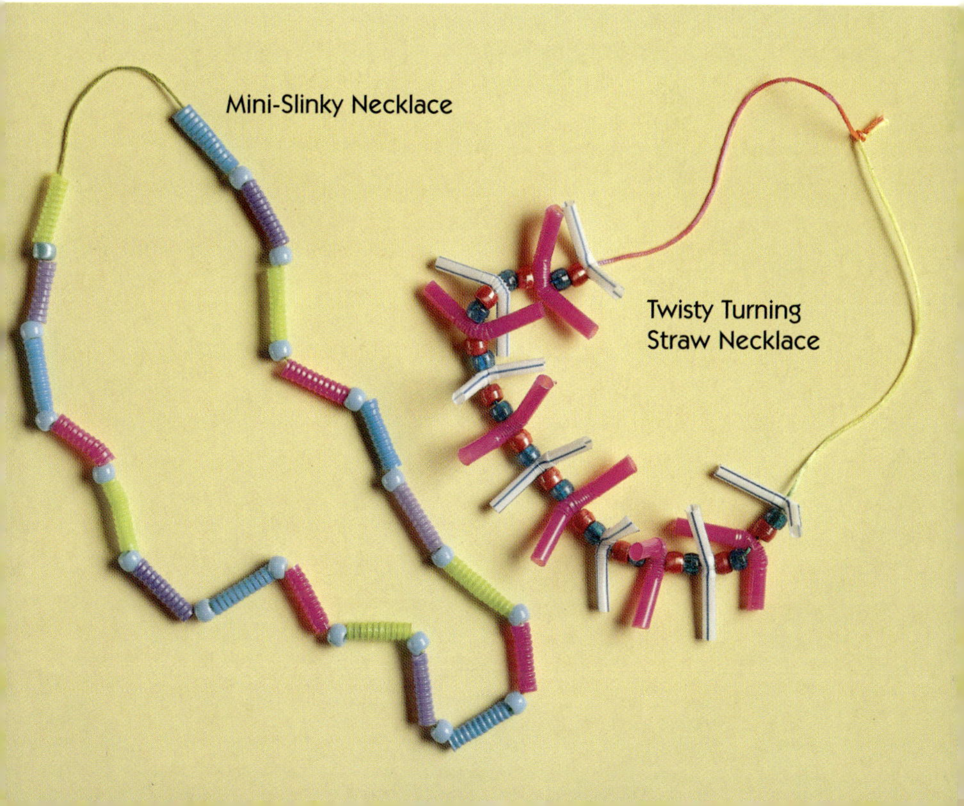
Twisty Turning
Straw Necklace

Balloon Buddy
Hot Glue Jewelry
Bad Hair
Day Pins
Funny Face Pins
Puffed Polka-Dot Shirt

Ready . . . Set . . . Create!

1. Wash and dry the shirt. This helps the paint to soak in better.
2. Slide the cardboard inside the shirt so the paint doesn't soak through.
3. If you are not using precut sponges, cut the sponges into shapes of stars and moons.
4. Pour the glow-in-the-dark paint in a disposable container.
5. Gently dip the sponge into the paint.
6. Press the sponge on the shirt. Keep repeating until the whole front of the shirt is covered with stars and moons.
7. Let the paint dry overnight.
8. Wear your glow-in-the-dark shirt to bed tomorrow night.

A tip from Sondra:
If you decide to add stars and moons to both the front and the back of the shirt, make sure the first side is completely dry before you do the second side.

Like astronomy? Check out the book
Crafts for Kids Who Are Wild About Outer Space,
by Kathy Ross (Millbrook Press).

SONDRA'S SUPER SOCKS

Sondra Says:

"It's fun to transform ordinary socks into extra-special super socks. You can just use odds and ends you have around the house."

Official Supply List

Beads and/or buttons

Needle and thread

Scissors (to cut thread after sewing)

Pair of plain-colored socks that cuff

Scrap cardboard

Fabric paint

Paintbrush

Ready . . . Set . . . Create!

1. Select some beads or buttons to be the flowers.
2. Use the needle and thread to sew the beads or buttons about 3 inches down from the top edge of each sock's cuff.
3. Slip a piece of cardboard inside each sock so the paint doesn't soak through.
4. Use fabric paint to paint stems and leaves beneath each button flower.
5. Let the paint dry and wear your socks with pride!

A tip from Sondra:
Experiment how far below the cuff to sew the buttons. It makes a difference if you plan to wear the socks pulled up, or with the cuff folded over.

Use old socks to make a cute "sock critter." For detailed directions, write to: RIT, Box 307, Coventry, CT 06238.

FOOTPRINT DEER SHIRT

Sondra Says:

"I made one of these shirts for my dad and wrote, 'You are my deerest dad!' underneath the deer. He wears it all the time."

Official Supply List

Scrap cardboard

Light-colored T-shirt or sweatshirt

Dark brown and beige fabric paints

2 disposable plastic containers

Thick paintbrush

Newspaper

Black permanent marker

Ready . . . Set . . . Create!

1. Slip cardboard inside the shirt so the paint doesn't soak through.
2. Lay the shirt on a hard flat surface.
3. Pour the fabric paint into the disposable containers (one color per container).
4. Take off your shoes and socks. Ask a friend or adult to paint the bottom of your foot with the beige paint.

Watch out! It will tickle. Make sure the bottom of your
foot is completely covered with paint.

5. Practice placing your foot on newspaper to see if you
   have too much or too little paint on your foot. You
   want to get a clear imprint of your foot.
6. Stand in front of the shirt so the bottom of the shirt is
   by your feet.
7. Press your foot on the center of the shirt, with your
   toes pointing toward the shirt's neck.
8. Lift your foot. The imprint is the head of your deer.
9. Clean and dry your foot.
10. Have a friend paint the palms of both your hands dark
    brown.
11. Place your hands on the shirt so the heels of your
    hands touch the toe prints on the shirt. These
    imprints will be the antlers.
12. Let the paint dry.
13. Use the permanent marker to draw eyes and nostrils
    on your deer.

A tip from Sondra:
If you want to make this as a Christmas present,
just draw a red nose on your reindeer to make a
Rudolph shirt.

Michael's Craft Stores offer a Web site with crafts for kids.
Check it out at *www.michaels.com.*

FANTASTIC FLIP-FLOPS

(extra quick and easy)

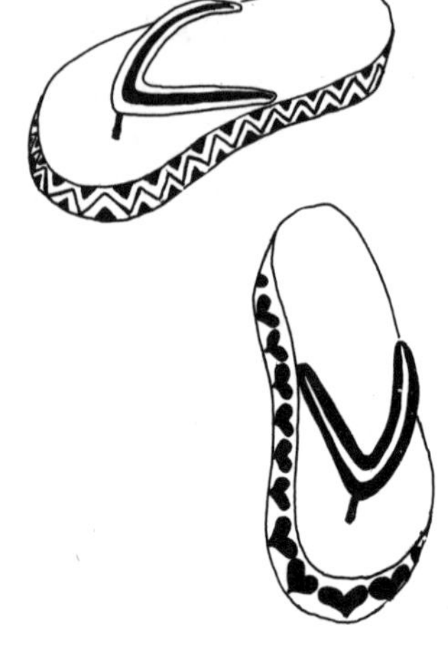

Sondra Says:

"You can paint these flip-flops to match the color of your swimsuit or beach towel."

Official Supply List

Newspaper

Rubber flip-flops with an embossed pattern on the straps

Permanent markers or fabric paint in a squeeze bottle

Ready . . . Set . . . Create!

1. Cover your work surface with newspaper.

2. Look closely at your flip-flops. They should have a design or pattern stamped into the rubber straps.

3. Simply use the permanent markers or fabric paint to decorate the pattern stamped on your flip-flop straps.

4. If using paint, let one color dry before you add another color.

5. If you're feeling extra creative, paint the edges of the flip-flops in a freehand design also.

A tip from Sondra:

Try to use white or light-colored flip-flops. Your paint will show up better and make a bolder design.

Lorianne Crook, host of the *Crook & Chase Show,*
a popular daytime talk show, told Sondra
that her favorite craft as a child was making trivets
for her mom out of glue and beans.

LADYBUG SOCKS

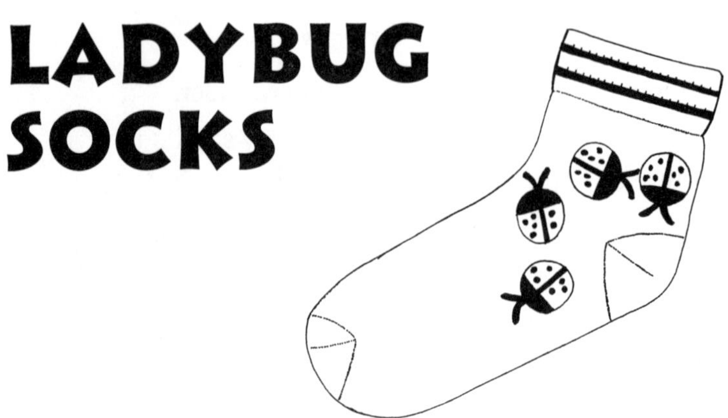

Sondra Says:

"It's fun to take an ordinary sock, add some paint, and create a whole new look for a summer outfit."

Official Supply List

Scrap cardboard

Solid-colored socks

Red fabric paint or red permanent marker

Pill-bottle cap or other round item, about 1 inch in diameter

Black permanent marker

Ready . . . Set . . . Create!

1. Slip a piece of cardboard inside each sock so the paint doesn't soak through.
2. Squeeze some red paint on another piece of scrap cardboard (unless you're using a marker).
3. Make sure the socks are lying flat, without wrinkles.
4. Dip the cap or other round item in the red paint, solid side down, or use the marker to trace the cap circle on the shirt and color it in.
5. Press the cap firmly on the sock to form a red circle.
6. Repeat 3 to 4 times until you have a nice pattern of ladybug bodies.
7. Repeat on the other sock.
8. Let the paint dry completely.
9. Turn the socks over and repeat.
10. After the paint dries, use the permanent marker to add antennas and spots on the back of the ladybugs.

A tip from Sondra:
Try to use a light-colored sock. The ladybugs will show up better with a pale background.

Oriental Trading Company offers a catalog full of inexpensive craft supplies. Have an adult call (800) 228-2269 for a free catalog or visit their Web site at *www.oriental.com*.

NO-SEW SILK FLOWER SHIRT

Sondra Says:

"This project sounds complicated, but after you do it once, you won't even need to look at the directions to do it again."

Official Supply List

Scrap cardboard

Plain-colored T-shirt

2 to 3 silk flowers with a few leaves

Iron and ironing board

¼ yard fusible webbing (available at low cost at fabric stores)

Scissors

Ready . . . Set . . . Create!

1. Place the cardboard inside the shirt and smooth out any wrinkles.

2. Here's the fun part! Pull the stem out of the silk flowers and leaves. You want to have only the flower part, without any wires or plastic.

3. Have an adult stand next to you as you use a warm iron to smooth out the silk flowers. They need to lay flat.

4. Place the rough or textured side of the fusible webbing on the back of your silk flower.

5. Iron the webbing for only 3 to 4 seconds. The heat melts the webbing to the flower, which can now be transferred to your shirt.

6. Trim away any extra webbing from the flower.

7. Peel off the paper attached to the webbing material.

8. Decide where you want your flower to be on the shirt. Simply place it with the "glue" side down on the fabric. Iron the flower for 35 to 40 seconds.

9. Turn the shirt over and iron for the same amount of time on the other side over the area where you placed the flower.

10. Your flower is now permanently attached. Repeat the process, adding or layering the leaves and flowers however you want.

A tip from Sondra:
Make sure an adult is right next to you when you use the iron, or let an adult do all the ironing while you supervise!

If you like making crafts with a friend,
look at *Super Friendship Crafts,* by Sharon McCoy
(Lowell House Publishing).

BUZZY BUZZY BEE SHIRT

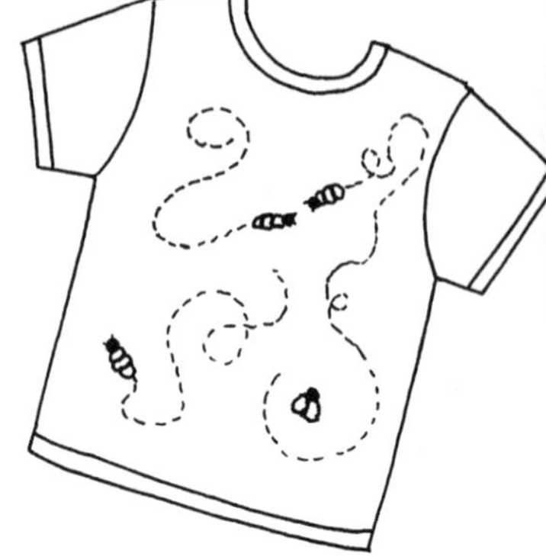

Sondra Says:

"Here's a way to have a bee on your shirt and never worry about getting stung."

Official Supply List

Several 1-inch yellow pom-poms

Scissors

Washable glue

T-shirt or sweatshirt, any color except yellow

Needle with large eye

Black embroidery floss

¼-inch black pom-poms (same number as large yellow ones)

Tiny wiggle eyes or white correction fluid

Ready . . . Set . . . Create!

1. Hold the yellow pom-pom between your thumb and forefinger, pinching it in half.

2. Use scissors to trim the pom-pom "fur" between your fingers (this will make the pom-pom look more like a bee; it also helps the black floss show up better as the bee stripes).

3. Dab a bit of glue on the shaggy, or untrimmed, side of the pom-pom.

4. Place the pom-pom on your shirt, glue side down, wherever you want the bee to sit.

5. Thread the needle with black embroidery floss.

6. Poke the needle through the shirt from the back side, right under the middle of the pom-pom. Bring the floss up and over the bee's "stomach," forming a stripe.

7. Bring the needle back through the shirt. Repeat two more times, so the bee has three stripes on her back. Tie a knot in the thread when you are finished.

8. You may need to trim the "fur" a little, so the black stripes are more distinctive.

9. Glue the small black pom-pom above the yellow pom-pom on the shirt. This is the bee's head.

10. Glue scraps of embroidery floss on the head to make antennas.

11. If you have tiny wiggle eyes, carefully glue those on the head. You can also use two drops of white correction fluid to make two small white eyes.

12. Make several bees flying on your shirt.

A tip from Sondra:
Be careful when you trim the fur on the pom-pom.
You don't want to cut the whole thing in half!

You can get lots more ideas for craft projects from Hot Off the Press Publishing. Have an adult call them at (888) 326-7255, or visit their Web site at *www.craftpizazz.com*.

CRAYON PRINT SHIRT

Sondra Says:

"You'll get the best results if you draw a simple design and use bright colors."

Official Supply List

Fabric crayons (available in most craft stores)

Plain piece of white paper

Light-colored shirt

Iron and ironing board

Scrap cardboard

Black permanent marker

Ready . . . Set . . . Create!

1. Draw a colorful picture on the paper with the fabric crayons.* Press down firmly, because darker colors show up best.

2. Put the shirt on the ironing board.

3. Set the iron to medium heat.

4. Slip a piece of cardboard inside the shirt. This stops the colors from soaking through.

5. Smooth out any wrinkles.

6. Turn the paper, design side down, on the shirt.

7. Have an adult iron over the paper. It's best to press down firmly, rather than sliding the iron back and forth. The heat will melt the crayon picture onto your shirt.

8. Remove the paper.

9. Turn off the iron.

10. For best results, outline your design with a black permanent marker.

*If you have trouble creating your own picture, you may like the patterns on pages 184 and 185.

A tip from Sondra:
If you write anything in your design, be sure to write the letters backwards on the paper. Then when you iron it on the shirt, the letters appear in the correct direction.

Most book or craft stores carry the magazine *Crafty Kids*. You'll like the colorful pictures that help you make stenciled T-shirts, gifts, and crafts.

SPRUCED-UP OVERALLS

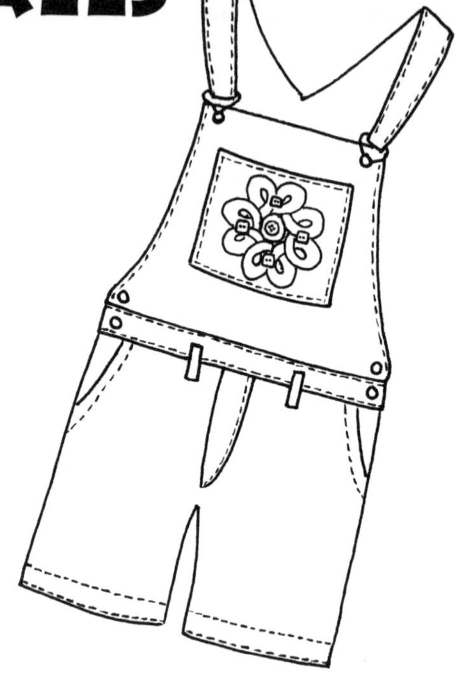

Sondra Says:

"You can transform an ordinary pair of overalls by simply adding a doily and some beads or buttons."

Official Supply List

Lace doily, 3 to 4 inches in diameter

Overalls or overall jumper

Needle and thread

Scissors (for cutting after you sew)

Assortment of beads or buttons

Ready . . . Set . . . Create!

1. Place the doily on the "bib" section on the front of your overalls.

2. Sew the doily onto the overalls. Make sure you sew the edges down.

3. Lay the beads or buttons on the doily. Experiment with a design. When you know where you want the beads or buttons to go, sew them on.

4. That's all! You've just designed a pair of custom overalls.

A tip from Sondra:
If you're not used to sewing, see if an adult has a thimble. This might save you from poking your finger.

Interested in sewing? The Home Sewing Association has ideas for easy kids' projects. See *www.sewing.org.*

SPREADING COLOR DESIGN SHIRT

Sondra Says:

"My favorite part of this craft is experimenting on an old shirt. I make 20 to 30 designs until I get a color combination I like."

Official Supply List

Scrap fabric

Scrap cardboard or newspaper

Permanent markers in assorted colors

Eyedropper

Rubbing alcohol

Light-colored cotton shirt

Ready . . . Set . . . Create!

1. Practice steps 1 through 8 on a piece of scrap fabric.
2. Lay a piece of cardboard or newspaper between the layers of fabric so the colors don't soak through.
3. With a permanent marker, draw four dots, about the size of a raisin, in a square, about 1 inch apart.
4. Use a different color marker and draw dots between the dots you just drew. Make the dots so they are almost touching.
5. Fill the eyedropper with rubbing alcohol.
6. Drop 2 to 3 drops of alcohol in the center of your dots.
7. Wait 30 to 60 seconds. Watch how the colors spread to make a design.
8. Experiment with different color combinations. You can even use 4 to 5 different colors
9. When you find a pattern you like, follow all these steps on your shirt. You could make a design on just the pocket, or all over the entire shirt.

A tip from Sondra:
Make sure an adult is with you when you use rubbing alcohol. Be careful not to get any in your eye because it really stings! Try this out on other things like overalls, socks, and even canvas tennis shoes.

Kids Crafts magazine gives ideas on many craft projects, including different ways to decorate shirts. It's available in most craft stores, or see *www.krause.com*.

DO-IT-YOURSELF VEST

(extra quick and easy)

Sondra Says:

"It's easy to change the look of an ordinary vest by adding new buttons and trims."

Official Supply List

Plain vest (denim always looks cute)

Assortment of buttons, bows, and ribbon flowers

> (You can usually get a whole packet at a craft store for under $2.00.)

Tape

Needle and thread

Scissors (for cutting after you sew)

Ready . . . Set . . . Create!

1. Lay the vest on a flat surface.

2. Experiment with placing your buttons, bows, and ribbons on the collar, pocket, etc.

3. When you get a design you like, tape the items in place. That way you can sew one on without forgetting how your design looked.

4. Simply sew on new decorative buttons, bows, or ribbon flowers.

A tip from Sondra:
Check your local thrift store to purchase a vest at a low cost. By the time you finish sewing on the fancy buttons, the vest will look like you got it at an expensive boutique.

The Muppets Big Book of Crafts by Stephanie St. Pierre (Workman Publishing) has over 100 different craft ideas. The color pictures help you follow the directions.

PUFFED POLKA-DOT SHIRT

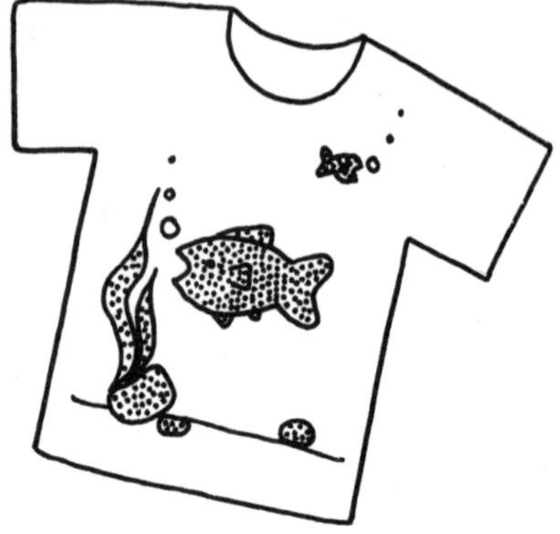

Sondra Says:

"It's fun to feel all the dots on this shirt after the paint dries."

Official Supply List

T-shirt or sweatshirt

Scrap cardboard

Pencil

2 to 3 colors of fabric paint

Paintbrush and paper plate for each color if fabric paint is
   not in squeezable bottles

Ready . . . Set . . . Create!

1. Lay the shirt on a flat surface.
2. Slip a piece of cardboard inside the shirt so the paint
   doesn't soak through.

3. Use a pencil to lightly draw a design or animal on
   your shirt.* Keep the picture fairly simple for best
   results. Try sketching something like a flower, a
   sailboat, or a fish.

4. If your fabric paint comes in a squeezable bottle,
   gently squeeze out "dots" all along the outline of your
   design. If you have regular fabric paint, just pour the
   paint on a paper plate and use the plastic end of a
   paintbrush dipped in the paint to make "dots."

5. Continue using the paint until you fill in your entire
   design, or certain sections, with polka dots.

6. After the main dotted design is finished, use the fabric
   paint and a paintbrush to add details to your picture,
   such as waves, trees, or the sun.

7. Let the shirt dry overnight before wearing. The dots of
   paint will harden and feel like firm bumps or "puffs."

*If you need help creating a picture, use the patterns on pages 186 and 187.

A tip from Sondra:
Practice making dots on a piece of scrap material
until you get them even in shape and size.

Hands On Crafts For Kids is a series of craft books, as
well as a PBS television program. For information, ask an
adult to call, or visit the Web site at *www.crafts4kids.com*.

GIANT FLOWER SHIRT

Sondra Says:

"Your friends will probably never guess you got the daisy design from a paper-plate holder!"

Official Supply List

Light-colored shirt (washed)

Scrap cardboard

Plastic paper-plate holder with spokes

Fabric paint (one color)

Tuna can or other shallow container

Sponge

Another color of fabric paint (optional)

Paintbrush (optional)

Needle and thread (optional)

2 small buttons (optional)

Permanent black marker (optional)

Ready . . . Set . . . Create!

1. Lay out the shirt on a hard flat surface.
2. Slip a piece of cardboard inside the shirt so the paint doesn't soak through.

3. Set the plastic paper-plate holder on top of the shirt, wherever you want your big flower to be. This is your giant stencil.

4. Ask a friend or adult to steady the holder firmly in one place.

5. Pour 1 to 2 tablespoons of paint into the tuna can or other container.

6. Dip the sponge in the paint and dab it on the material showing through the paper-plate holder. Try not to move the "stencil."

7. Keep dabbing the paint on the shirt until all the "slots" are filled in.

8. Carefully lift the paper-plate holder off the shirt.

9. Let the paint dry.

10. If you want, paint the center of your flower a contrasting color. Add leaves and a flower stem, or just leave the flower as it is.

11. Sew on buttons as eyes to give your flower a face. Draw a nose and mouth with a permanent marker.

A tip from Sondra:
Dense cosmetic sponges work well for stenciling because they don't spread paint under the stencil. You can usually find them at dollar stores.

> Cozie Kids is a brand that carries great canvas aprons, storage bags, and even bucket covers designed to let you store craft supplies. Plus you can decorate the canvas! Visit the Web site at *www.headstarts.com*.

FABRIC STAMP SHIRT

(extra quick and easy)

Sondra Says:

"Many craft stores carry this type of fabric stamp. They are usually made of foam and have clear, distinct designs. Best of all, they usually cost less than a dollar."

Official Supply List

Light-colored T-shirt or sweatshirt

Scrap cardboard

Paintbrush

2 to 3 colors of fabric paint

Fabric stamp

Ready . . . Set . . . Create!

1. Wash the shirt to remove the sizing.

2. Lay the shirt on a hard flat surface.

3. Slip a piece of cardboard inside the shirt so the paint doesn't soak through.

4. Using a paintbrush, apply fabric paint to a section of the fabric stamp.

5. Use another color or colors to paint the remaining section. For example, if your stamp is of a flower, you could paint the stem green and the flower portion red.

6. Firmly press the stamp on the shirt.

7. Lift the stamp straight up so the paint doesn't smear.

8. Repeat the process by adding more paint to the stamp and then making designs on the shirt.

9. Let the paint dry before you wear the shirt.

A tip from Sondra:
It helps to have a friend or adult hold the shirt down as you lift up the stamp. That way you'll get a clear design.

Anita's Fabric Stamps have deep grooved designs to help you get great results when decorating your T-shirts. Ask an adult to call (678) 206-7373 for information.

FLOWER POWER SHOES

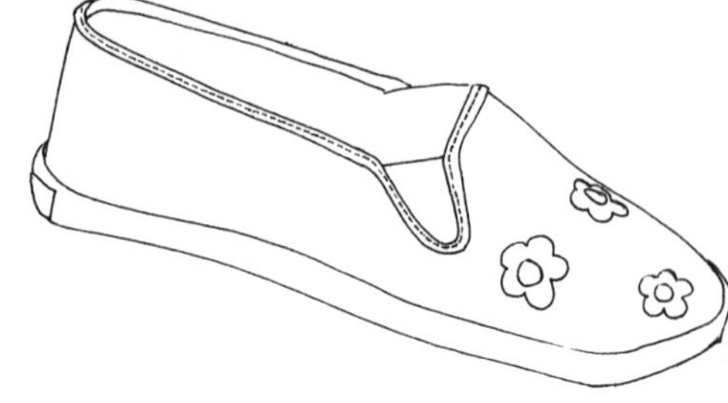

Sondra Says:

"It's fun to see how an ordinary pencil eraser can make decorative flowers on your shoes."

Official Supply List

2 to 3 colors of fabric paint, in colors that contrast with
  the canvas shoes

Scrap cardboard

Pencil with a new eraser on the end

Pair of solid-colored canvas shoes

Ready . . . Set . . . Create!

1. Pour a small amount of fabric paint on a piece of cardboard.
2. Gently dip the eraser end of the pencil in the paint.
3. Make a "dot" on your shoe by bringing the painted eraser straight down onto it, then lifting it straight off.
4. Make another dot next to it, so the sides are barely touching.
5. Continue making dots, until you have five dots.
6. Use a different color of paint for the center of the flower.
7. Decorate both shoes with as many multicolored flowers as you like.
8. Let the paint dry.

A tip from Sondra:
For best results and to keep the colors from blending, let the paint dry before you add another color to the flower center.

Your computer can help with craft projects.
Check out *Creative Crafts and Gifts'* software program.
It has patterns for tote bags, pillows, and pouches.
See *www.dogbyte.com.*

FABRIC PAINTED SWEATSHIRT OR T-SHIRT

(extra quick
and easy)

Sondra Says:

"This shirt is inexpensive to make if you buy your shirt at a thrift store or garage sale."

Official Supply List

Scrap paper

Pencil

Scrap cardboard

Plain-colored sweatshirt or T-shirt

Squeezable fabric paint

Ready . . . Set . . . Create!

1. Use the scrap paper and pencil to sketch out a design you like.*

2. Lay a piece of cardboard inside the shirt so the paint doesn't come through.

3. Lightly sketch the design you made onto the shirt.

4. Now simply use the fabric paint to cover over the pencil lines to finish your picture.

5. Let the paint dry according to the fabric paint instructions.

*If you need help sketching a design, use the patterns on pages 188 and 189.

A tip from Sondra:
If you want to add a sparkly effect to your shirt, sprinkle some glitter on the wet paint. It will stick to the paint and shine.

Fabric BLOpens are virtual air brushes used to decorate fabric. Ten colors let you create pretty designs and patterns. See *www.blopens.com.*

NO-SEW APPLIQUÉ SHIRT

Sondra Says:

"With just a scrap of colorful fabric, you can change an ordinary shirt into something special."

Official Supply List

Scissors

Scrap material that has distinct "pictures" such as teddy bears, flowers, dogs, etc.

¼ yard of fusible webbing (available at low cost at fabric stores)

Iron and ironing board

Plain-colored T-shirt or sweatshirt (washed)

Squeezable fabric paint (optional)

Ready . . . Set . . . Create!

1. Carefully cut out the design from your fabric.
2. Place the rough or textured side of the fusible webbing on the *back* of your material piece.

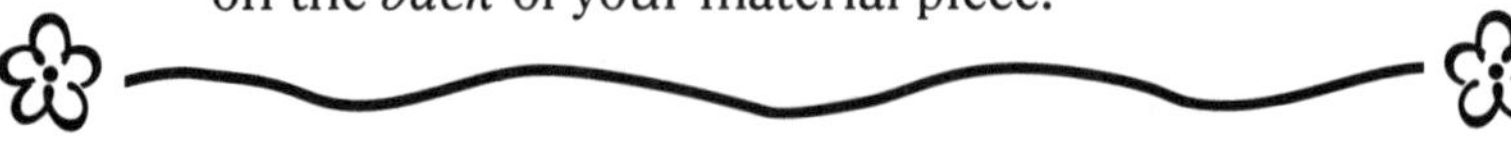

3. With an adult nearby, iron the fusible webbing for 3 to
   4 seconds. The heat melts the webbing to the material,
   which now can be transferred to your shirt.

4. Trim away any extra webbing from your fabric.

5. Peel off the paper attached to the webbing.

6. Decide where you want the fabric piece to be on your
   shirt. Simply place it, webbing side down, on the shirt.
   Iron the fabric for 35 to 40 seconds.

7. Turn the shirt over and iron for 35 to 40 seconds on
   the other side over the area where you placed the
   design.

8. The fabric piece is now permanently attached to the
   shirt. If you want, use fabric paint to cover the edges
   of the fabric or embellish the pattern.

9. Repeat the process for all the designs you want to use.

A tip from Sondra:
Practice with some scraps of fusible webbing and
fabric to get the best results before you work on
your shirt.

For a complete listing and sample assortment of *free* craft
project sheets, send $1 (postage and handling) and a long,
self-addressed envelope to Cindy Groom-Harry, Depart-
ment S-Book, 2363 460th Street, Ireton, IA 51027.

SPLATTER-DRIP SHIRT

Sondra Says:

"This paint design really changes when you hang up the wet shirt."

Official Supply List

Water

One cotton shirt, prewashed

Coat hanger

2 to 3 colors of fabric paint

2 to 3 spray bottles

Ready . . . Set . . . Create!

1. Wet the shirt, then wring out excess water.

2. Put the shirt on the coat hanger so it is ready to hang up.

3. Lay the shirt on the grass or sidewalk.

4. Put 1 to 2 teaspoons paint in each spray bottle.

5. Add 2 teaspoons water to each spray bottle.

6. Shake bottles to mix the paint and water.

7. Spray the wet shirt with the spray bottle, any design you want.

8. Use all of the colors of paint.

9. Turn the shirt over and do the same on the back side.

10. When you have a colorful design, hang the wet shirt on a tree or some place outside.

11. Wait about 5 minutes and watch how the colors streak down into long teardrop shapes.

12. When you get a design you like, lay the shirt on a flat surface to dry.

13. Let your friends guess how you got the colors to "streak."

A tip from Sondra:
This project works best on a sunny day when you can let your shirt dry outside on the grass.

There are lots of ideas for hair clips and other crafts on the Lisa Frank Web site: *www.lisafrank.com.*

FLYING APPLE BUTTERFLY SHIRT

Sondra Says:

"You've probably printed with apples before. Now turn your apple print into a colorful butterfly."

Official Supply List

Solid-colored, washed T-shirt or sweatshirt

Scrap cardboard

1 color of brush-on fabric paint

Paper plate for paint

1 apple, cut in half

2 to 3 colors of "puff" paint in a squeeze bottle

Ready . . . Set . . . Create!

1. Lay the shirt on a smooth hard surface.
2. Place the cardboard inside the shirt so the paint doesn't soak through.
3. Pour about 1 tablespoon fabric paint on paper plate.
4. Dip the apple, cut side down, in the paint. Make sure it is covered with paint.
5. Press the paint-covered apple on your shirt. These are the wings of your butterfly.
6. Repeat the process for as many "butterflies" as you want.
7. Let the paint dry.
8. After the paint dries, use the squeeze bottles of paint to draw designs on the wings and add antennas.
9. As soon as the second batch of paint dries, put on your butterfly shirt and eat the unpainted half of the apple.

A tip from Sondra:
When you cut the apple in half, start cutting from the top where the stem is. If you cut the apple in half around the "middle," you'll get a different shape than butterfly wings.

We all love free items. Check out the book
Free Stuff for Crafty Kids on the Internet, by Judy Heim and Gloria Hansen (C&T Publishing).

LAZY DAISY JEANS

Sondra Says:

"This is a good project to do when you are learning to embroider. You can make as many daisies as you want."

Official Supply List

Assorted colors embroidery floss

Embroidery needle with large eye

One pair jeans, jean shorts, or a jean skirt

Scissors

Fabric glue (optional)

Small beads

Ready . . . Set . . . Create!

1. Thread the floss through the needle and tie a knot at the end.

2. Starting on the underneath side of your jeans, bring the needle up until the knot stops the thread.

3. Bring the needle down right next to where you just came through the material. This forms a "loop" with the floss.

4. As you keep pulling the floss, the loop gets smaller. When the loop is about ½ inch long, stop pulling.

5. Follow the diagram to see how to make a small stitch at the end of your loop. You just made your first flower petal. Make four to five petals for each flower.*

6. When you complete one flower, tie a knot on the underside of your skirt and cut the floss.

7. Make as many flowers as you want.

8. Sew or glue on tiny beads in the center of each flower.

*See the daisy diagram on page 190 to help you make your daisy for these jeans.

A tip from Sondra:
If you've never tried embroidery before, practice on a piece of scrap material. This stitch is very easy once you've done it a few times.

You'll find hundreds of creative craft projects on *www.craftclick.com*. They offer ideas for clay projects, holiday crafts, and gifts to make.

IRON-ON TRANSFER SHIRT

Sondra Says:

"This shirt ends up looking like something you would buy in a store. It's special though, because you made it."

Official Supply List

Towel

One solid-colored, washed shirt

Iron

Scissors

Iron-on transfer(s) (available at any craft store)

Ready . . . Set . . . Create!

1. Place the towel on a hard surface, like a kitchen counter.

2. Put the shirt on top of the towel. Smooth out any wrinkles.

3. With an adult next to you, set the iron on the hottest setting and iron the shirt.

4. Use the scissors to trim away any extra white paper around your transfer, leaving about a ½-inch border.

5. Place the transfer, colorful side down, on the shirt.

6. Cover with the parchment paper that comes in your package.

7. Again, make sure an adult is next to you while you firmly press the iron-on the transfer. It takes about 25 to 30 seconds for the picture to transfer to the shirt.

8. Carefully peel back a corner section of the transfer. If it isn't sticking to the shirt yet, iron for another 10 to 15 seconds.

9. Turn the iron off and remove the backing from the transfer. You should have a colorful design on your shirt.

10. Be sure to let the shirt cool down before you put it on!

A tip from Sondra:
Don't use an ironing board for this project. A very hard surface is needed for the iron to transfer the pattern to the shirt.

Always remember to keep your craft area clean.
You don't want to slip on a paint bottle while holding a container of tiny seed beads!

Chapter Five

Wearable Odds and Ends

EMBOSSED VELVET MATERIAL

Sondra Says:

"You'll enjoy using this technique to embellish the velvet. Then make a purse, book cover, or a hair scrunchie with your piece of velvet."

Official Supply List

Fabric stamp with distinct shapes

Smooth piece of wood, bigger than a piece of typing paper at least

Piece of velvet about ½ a yard, depending on what you want to make (Velvet labeled rayon/acetate works best.)

Spray bottle with water

Iron

Ready . . . Set . . . Create!

1. Lay your fabric stamp, design side up, on the wooden board. If you iron on an ironing board, you won't get as clear a design, because the cushioning is too soft.
2. Place the velvet, with the fuzzy side down, on top of the stamp.
3. Spray the fabric with 2 to 3 squirts of water. The material should be wet but not saturated.
4. With an adult nearby, heat the iron to the hottest setting and firmly press the hot iron on top of the fabric and stamp.
5. Hold in place for 20 seconds. Do not move the iron back and forth.
6. Remove the iron and enjoy the new pattern you created.
7. Use the fabric to make a purse, book cover, hair scrunchie, or something else.

A tip from Sondra:
Practice on a small piece of fabric to get the best results. If you don't have fabric stamps, cut shapes out of thick cardboard or even bend coat hangers into shapes to make the impressions on the fabric.

You can order a Roylco catalog that offers
hundreds of creative, low-cost craft items.
Have an adult contact them at (800) 362-8656.

SOME FUN THUMB ART

(Try saying that five times fast!)

Sondra Says:

"Here's one time it's okay to spread your fingerprints around!"

Official Supply List

Permanent ink pad

Scrap paper

Fine-tip permanent marker or fabric paint

Paintbrush if painting

White handkerchief or plain-colored scarf

Ready . . . Set . . . Create!

1. Put your thumb or pointer finger on the ink pad.
2. Press your finger firmly on the scrap paper to make a fingerprint. This is just to practice before putting the ink on your actual project.
3. Use the marker or paint to add details. How about making a roller-skating bug or a jumping jelly bean?
4. Put your finger in the ink again and then press it on a corner of the scarf or handkerchief. Try combining several prints to make a long caterpillar.
5. Use markers or paint to add personality to your fingerprints.
6. Make as many fingerprint creations as you like.

A tip from Sondra:
If you want to get really wild, make a print using your big toe!

Elmer's makes 3-D paint pens, Galactic Glue, and Tacky Paste. Check out their Web site for great craft projects at *www.elmers.com.*

BAKED RIBBON DELIGHTS

Sondra Says:

"This is a strange way to get ribbons to curl . . . but it works. Just don't get them mixed up with chocolate chip cookies you might be baking at the same time!"

Official Supply List

Thin fabric ribbon ¼ inch and/or ½ inch, in various colors, cut into ten 12-inch lengths

Water

Pencils (one for each 12-inch piece of ribbon)

Tape

Cookie sheet

Oven

Two 2-inch sections of pipe cleaners, any color.

Ready . . . Set . . . Create!

1. Wet the ribbons in water. Squeeze out excess water.
2. Wrap the wet ribbon tightly up and down a pencil; it's okay to overlap the ribbon a little bit. Use a piece of tape to prevent the ribbon from unwrapping at each end.
3. Place your ribbon-covered pencils on a cookie sheet.
4. Have an adult put the cookie sheet in the oven for 20 minutes at 225 degrees F.
5. Ask an adult to remove the cookie sheet after your ribbons have "baked."
6. Gently unwrap the ribbons for a curly treat.
7. Twist each piece of pipe cleaner around the center of five ribbons.
8. Use the pipe cleaner to attach a curly ribbon cluster to the first section of shoelaces on your shoes. If the ribbons are too long, so you might step on them, simply trim the ends.

A tip from Sondra:
You can use these ribbons to decorate hair clips or headbands also.

Consider making a large number of craft projects with some friends. Then organize a neighborhood crafts sale. You'll have fun making crafts, plus earn money!

BRIGHT AND BOUNCY BIRTHDAY HATS

Sondra Says:

"Instead of wearing those silly pointed birthday hats, have everyone at your party make their own unique hat."

Official Supply List

Strips of colored construction paper, 2 to 3 inches wide and at least 11 inches long

Stapler

Glue

Pipe cleaners, stickers, glitter, sequins, buttons, ribbon, and any other decorations

Scissors

Ready . . . Set . . . Create!

1. Measure the construction paper strips to fit around your head. Staple or glue the pieces together when you get the right size to make a "crown."

2. Using this paper headband as a base, start adding decorations. (Wrap pipe cleaners around pencils to create "curls," attach streamers of ribbon, glue on buttons or sequins, and get wild and add glitter.)

3. If it is your birthday, cut out a number showing how old you are and glue it to the front of your headband.

4. Stick it on your head and wear this bright and bouncy hat throughout the party.

A tip from Sondra:
This is a good activity for your friends to do while you're waiting for all the guests to arrive.

For more fun birthday party ideas for crafts, games, and food, look at Penny Warner's book. *Birthday Parties for Kids* (Prima Publishing).

SPARKLING WIZARD HAT

Sondra Says:

"This is a great project to make if you are going to a Harry Potter party."

Official Supply List

Scissors

16-by-16-inch piece of light cardboard or construction paper,

Pencil

Tape (optional)

Glue

Hot glue gun (optional)

Glitter and/or sequins

Sparkling stickers

Stencils (optional)

Ready . . . Set . . . Create!

1. Use a pencil to draw a fat pie shape on the cardboard or paper.
2. Cut along the line. This gives you the shape for your hat.*
3. Gently fold the sides of the cardboard together to make a cone shape.
4. Have someone adjust the bottom of the cone to fit your head.
5. Tape or glue the edges of the cone together.
6. If needed, trim the bottom of the hat to make it even.
7. Add glitter, sequins, and shiny stickers to your wizard hat.
8. If you want, place a star stencil on the hat. Fill in the space with glue, then sprinkle with glitter.
9. Put on your hat and get ready for a Quidditch match!

*Use the diagram on page 191 for help drawing and cutting the right shape.

A tip from Sondra:
If your hat doesn't stay on, simply punch two holes in the side of the wide end. Attach two pieces of ribbon to form a bow that ties under your chin.

A great glue to use for this project is Kids Choice Glue.
It comes in a tube and is extra thick so it works
inside the stencil for your wizard hat.
You can get it at *www.beacon1.com*.

SQUEAKY MOUSE HAT

Sondra Says:

"This mouse pattern is so easy to make, you can put mice all over your house."

Official Supply List

Scrap piece of paper

Pencil

Scissors

Pink felt or craft foam

White or gray felt or craft foam

Needle and embroidery floss

Wiggle eyes

Craft glue

Plain-colored cloth hat

Gray or black pipe cleaner, about 4 inches long

Yellow craft foam (optional)

Ready . . . Set . . . Create!

1. On a piece of paper, draw an egg shape about 3½ to 4 inches long.
2. Cut out the shape and use it to trace the egg shape on the pink felt or craft foam. This is your mouse body.
3. Carefully cut two 1-inch slits in the center of the foam, about ⅓ of the way back from the narrow end.*
4. Trace a number 8 on the white or gray felt, about 2½ inches high. Cut around the outside of the 8 to make the ears.
5. Slip the ears through the two slits on the mouse body.
6. Use the needle and embroidery floss to make the whiskers.
7. Glue on wiggle eyes.
8. Use the craft glue to glue the mouse body on the hat.
9. Spread glue on one side of the pipe cleaner and lay it near the back of the mouse for the tail.
10. If you like, add some yellow craft foam for cheese in case your mouse gets hungry.

*If you're confused about how to draw these shapes or cut the foam, refer to the diagrams on pages 192 and 193.

A tip from Sondra:
Feel free to use any color foam or felt to make your mouse. Everyone likes an orange mouse!

For some unique craft projects, try making things with industrial-strength cardboard from *www.kraftables.com*. You can even make and decorate a cardboard chair.

A FEW OTHER PROJECTS AND HELPFUL HINTS

- Get a plastic headband. Wrap pieces of colored tape around it for a multicolored headband.
- If you have a top with buttons, use fine-tipped color markers to draw stripes or polka dots on the buttons for a new look.
- Go to garage sales and buy inexpensive necklaces with interesting beads. Cut the necklaces apart and make your own jewelry.
- Use fabric paint to decorate a pair of plain tennis shoes.
- Weave a thin ribbon in and out of minipretzels for a handy snack around your neck.
- Have a "Craft Swap Party" with your friends. Ask everyone to bring paint, markers, glitter, and other supplies that they don't want. Then trade with each other. You'll all end up with "new" craft supplies.
- Make a mosaic print on a T-shirt. Simply cut a carrot in half and dip it in fabric paint. Use this stamp to create a picture.
- Remember to pull back long hair when working on a project. You don't want glue and glitter in your curls!

- An old shower curtain is great to put over a table so you don't have to worry about paint spills and glue drops.

- Ask your parents what crafts they did as a child. Make a project together.

- If you baby-sit, put together a kit to take with you filled with safe items. Include paper, washable markers, and ribbon. Let your little friends make creative masterpieces.

# HELPFUL ILLUSTRATIONS

SINGING IN THE RAIN
UMBRELLA PATTERNS

(continues)

VERY STRETCHY VISOR PATTERN

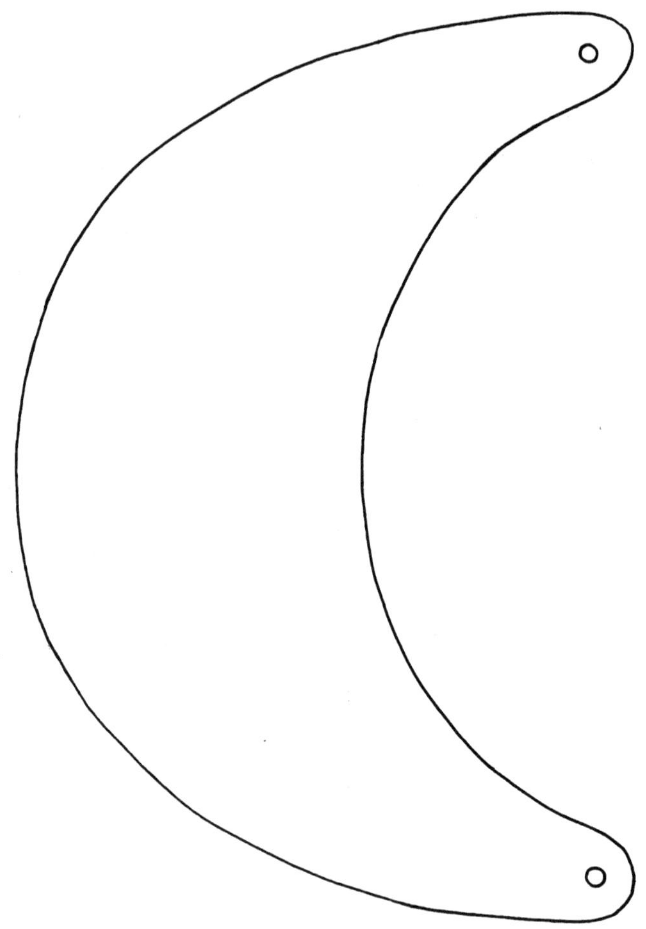

BABY'S HOMEMADE BIB DIAGRAM

SHRINKING GHOST NECKLACE PATTERNS

GLOW-IN-THE-DARK PJS PATTERNS

CRAYON PRINT SHIRT PATTERNS

PUFFED POLKA-DOT SHIRT PATTERNS

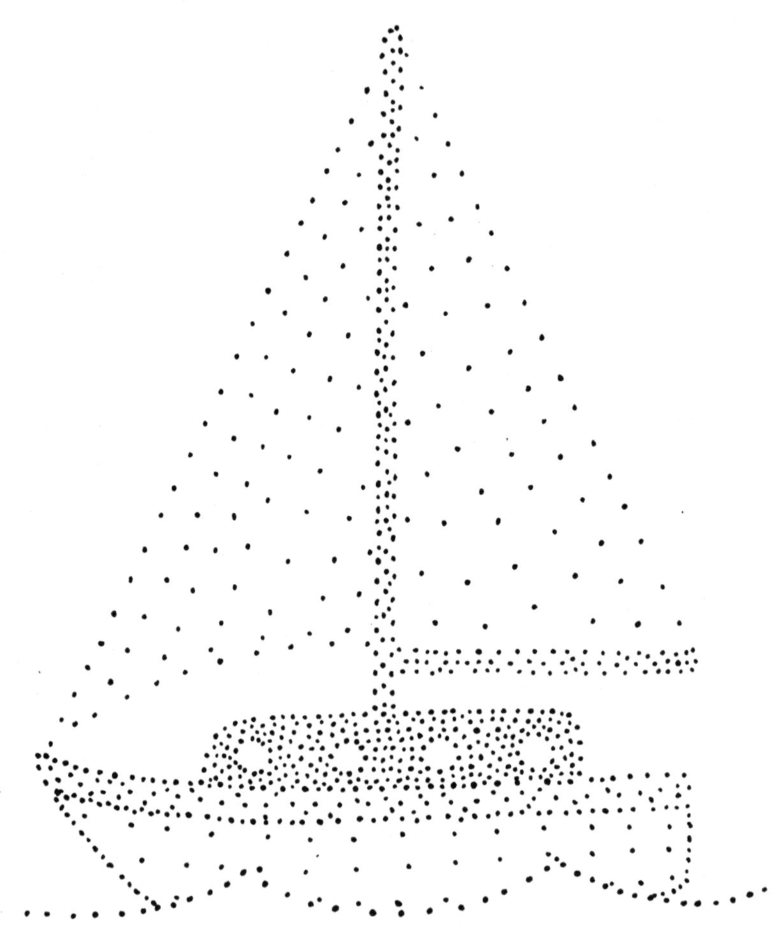

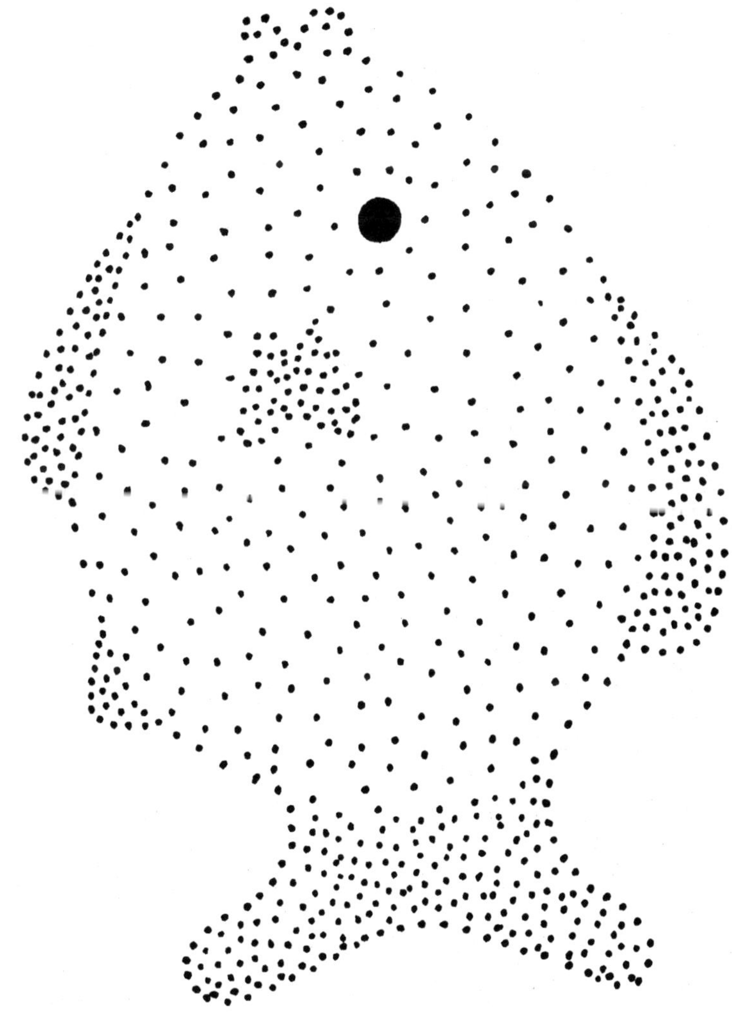

Helpful Illustrations • 187

FABRIC-PAINTED SWEATSHIRT OR T-SHIRT PATTERNS

LAZY DAISY JEANS DIAGRAM

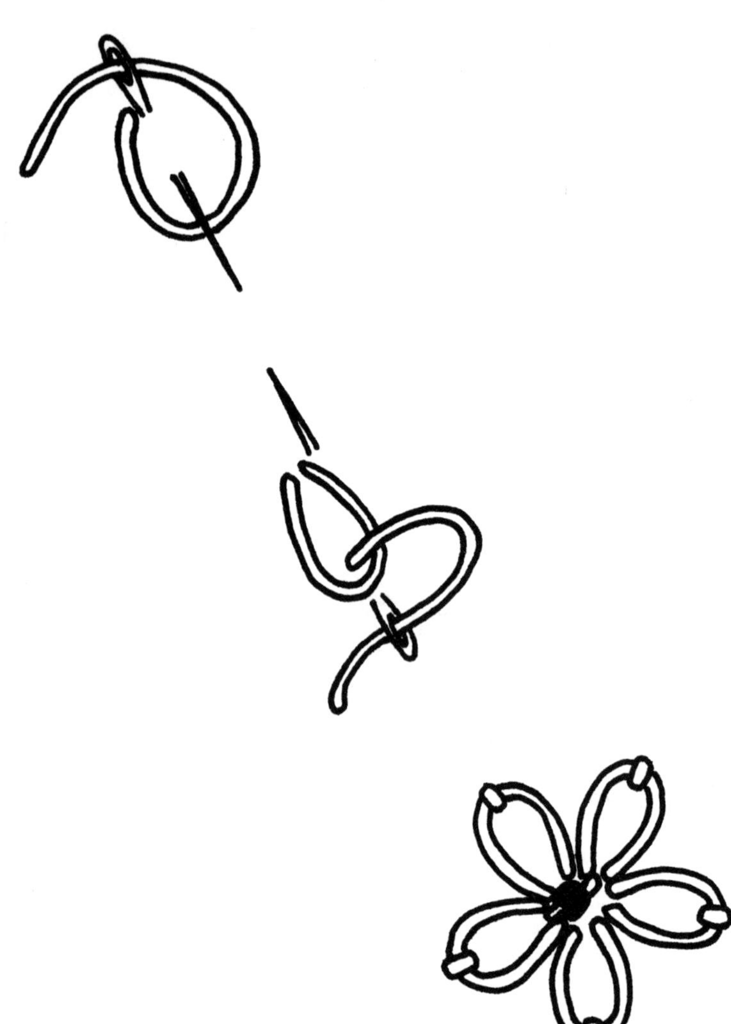

SPARKLING WIZARD HAT DIAGRAM

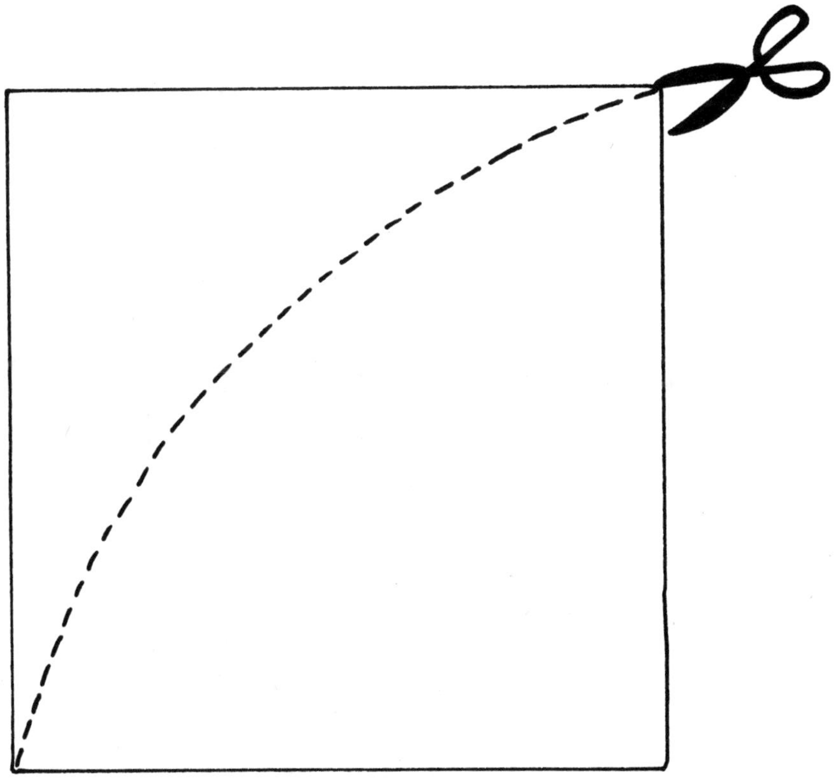

SQUEAKY MOUSE HAT DIAGRAMS

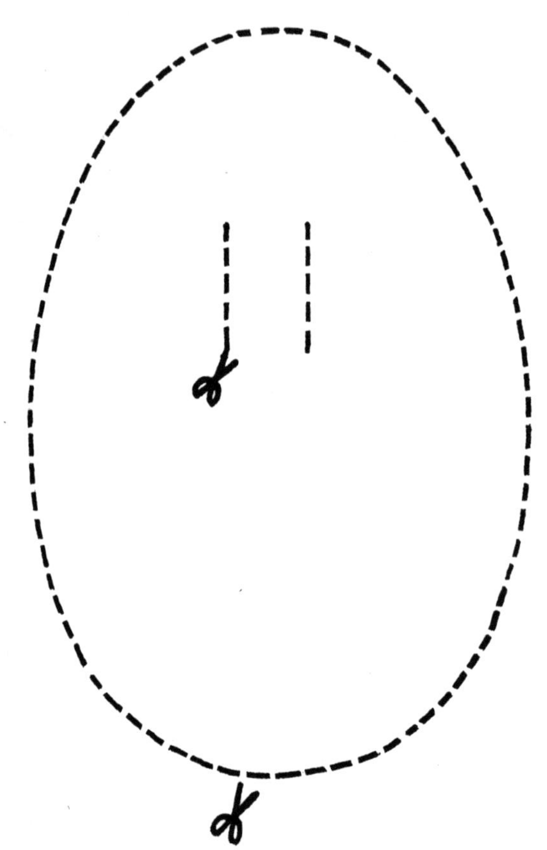

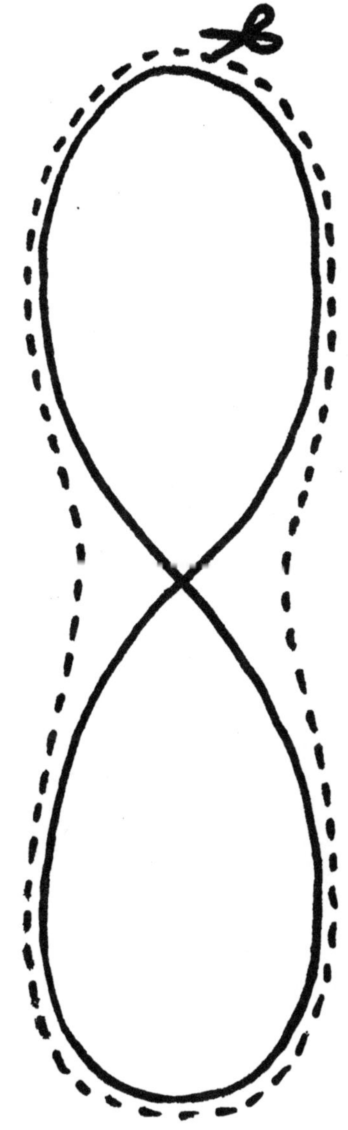